Recovery
Through
God's
Truth

Recovery Through God's Truth

STEVEN B. CURINGTON

Reformers Unanimous International

PO Box 15732, Rockford, IL 61132
Visit our website at www.reformu.com.
Printed in Canada
Cover design by Granite Creative, inc.

Curington, Steven B., 1965-
Recovery Through God's Truth / Steven Curington.

ISBN 978-0-615-39801-3

DEDICATION

Recovery Through God's Truth is dedicated to three men God used to shape my life.

The first man taught me the value of character and hard work. He is a great father who never gave up on me despite my many failures. He is the gentlest man I know. Without question, no person shaped my *personal life* more than my dad,

Delmar Curington.

The second man trained me to preach and taught me through example how to live the abundant Christian life. His confidence in me has been the driving force for the development of Reformers Unanimous. He is the most loving man I know. Without question, no person has shaped my *spiritual life* more than my pastor,

Paul Kingsbury.

The third man enlightened me in how to gain God's power on my life and in my work. He hired me despite my résumé saying I would be a waste of time. As my former employer, I still seek his wise counsel. He is the meekest man I know. Without question, no person has shaped my *professional life* more than my mentor,

Daniel Arnold.

ACKNOWLEDGMENTS

I am especially grateful to my wife, **Lori**. She never expressed frustration with my countless hours spent on this book.

Many thanks to the **RU editorial staff members** who have sacrificially given of their time, insight, and expertise to bring this project from bud to full bloom. This book would have remained an impossibility without them.

Additional thanks to **Steve Wamberg**, **Wendy Burks** and **Julie Kuss.**

In conclusion, I thank **God** for His gracious leading during the tenure of this book. My journey began with a desire to teach others about the abundant Christian life, only to find myself transformed as the Holy Spirit matured me to a position of enlightenment that has changed the way I view all my circumstances in life.

CONTENTS

FOREWORD

Do you feel empty, alone in your Christian walk and absent of the joy that is promised to God's people in His word? Has this frustration led you to feed appetites that you know are wrong but you struggle to overcome? If so, you are not alone. You are attempting to live freely in a bound world.

There is HOPE - a hope that is being hidden from believers in Christ. It is called the abundant Christian Life and it is available for all of God's people who will know their God.

Let *Recovery Through God's Truth* excite you as you learn the value of each and every circumstance that God intends to use for good so that you may grow spiritually and draw others to our Savior.

*May God bless you as we begin
our journey to freedom in
a bound world*

Through Christ Jesus, God Is for Me. Therefore, If God Is Against It, So Am I.

Jesus saith unto him, I am the way, the truth, and the life: no man cometh unto the Father, but by me. —John 14:6

Now the works of the flesh are manifest, which are these; Adultery, fornication, uncleanness, lasciviousness, Idolatry, witchcraft, hatred, variance, emulations, wrath, strife, seditions, heresies, envyings, murders, drunkenness, revelings and such like: of the which I tell you before, as I have also told you in time past, that they which do such things shall not inherit the kingdom of God.

Galatians 5:19-21

The Bible was written to tell us what is right, what is not right, how to get right and how to stay right. If God's intention was to inform us of what is, what is not, how to get and how to stay right, then it is our responsibility to conform each area of our lives that is revealed to be wrong. That is the truth behind the second part of this chapter's principle: *If God's against it, so am I.*

But we can't conform our lives to God's will on our own. God will help us do this. He gives new believers His Spirit and a hunger to be right. God wants us to succeed in obedience to Him. He is ready to help us draw the lines of behavior that both please Him and help us move forward. Indeed, *God is for me.*

God uses this new presence and new desire for good to mold our new Christian character. If we draw a line and do not overstep this line of behavior that is considered by God to be wrong, then He will reveal more and more things that He would like to change in our lives. As we continue to adopt these revelations of God's will for us, we will find ourselves further and further from the original line (which is to not indulge in our addiction). Eventually, we will find ourselves so far from our original line in the sand, so to speak, that even when we have a bad day, the thought of using or engaging in our addiction is not even a remote possibility. This is a joyous place to be!

But how do we get to that place? Back to this chapter's principle: *through Christ Jesus.* Christ is the proof that God is for us! Consider the great truth of Romans 5:8: *But God commendeth his love toward us, in that, while we were yet sinners, Christ died for us.* Before we even knew enough about God to love and obey Him, God provided the payment for our sin through Christ Jesus. He made Christ the Way, the Truth, and the Life.

This is why, right now, we must take the time to introduce readers to the single most important Person in our recovery process. It is not you. It is not your spouse or sponsor, or even your support group. It is our Savior Jesus Christ. In this chapter, we are going to discover how freedom is found by following this Way, Truth, and Life. We will look at God's truth that leads to freedom versus the lie of the world that leads to bondage.

Through Christ Jesus, God is for me. Therefore, if God is against it, so am I.

Jesus, the Way

Society will tell us there are many different ways to overcome an addiction. In my search while away from God, I learned many of them as I attempted my road to recovery in my own power. I tried to overcome my addictions without God's way to freedom. In other words, the problem with these is that they are poor substitutes for Jesus Christ!

SELF-HELP PROGRAMS

The first way society guides us to freedom is through self-help programs. This way teaches that we must think more highly of ourselves, that we must improve our low self-esteem and negative self-image. I personally struggled with addiction for over ten years. I sought counsel from a variety of society's programs. Nearly every time I was told that I had low self-esteem; I had a low opinion of myself. What solution did they offer? I needed to think more highly of myself! I needed to realize that I was a good man for making an effort. By being proud of my accomplishments, I would overcome my strongholds.

As a result of this mistaken philosophy, I remained addicted for many years. I had come to believe that if I only thought more of myself, I could be like the others who had been set free from their addictions. This way failed, and failed, and failed. It seemed as if the more I tried it, the harder I fell.

Why did this way fail? When I would begin to feel better about myself, and become proud of my accomplishment of temporary sobriety, and experience any real clean time, I always seemed to stumble shortly thereafter. The reason for my failure is found in Proverbs

16:18: *Pride goeth before destruction, and a haughty spirit before a fall.* The principle being taught here is that if we believe in ourselves to do something that only God can do for us, we will stumble and eventually be destroyed through our self-centered efforts. Proverbs 29:23 reminds us that, *A man's pride shall bring him low.*

A second mistake with this self-focused philosophy is that this advice was coming from men who were not seeking the ways of the Lord. Proverbs 14:12 says, *There is a* way *which seemeth right unto a man, but the end thereof are the ways of death.* That was part of my problem! I was seeking counsel from men whose motives were good, and although they wanted to help me, their advice was not coming from the Lord. According to this Proverbs 14 verse, the ways of man will look right, but the end result will be a premature death. That wasn't the result I was looking for, and I think it's safe to say you aren't either.

What is God's answer to these philosophical errors? First, seek godly counsel. Since man's way and man's advice lead to death (a spiritual and sometimes a premature physical death), we should seek advice from people who get their counsel from God.

Second, we must reject our self-centered pride and be willing to humble ourselves. It was a glorious day when I got down on my knees and said, "Oh, God, I can't do it by myself! I need your help, Lord! Please help me overcome this habit!" When I was willing to humble myself in the sight of the Lord, then He was willing to lift me up. I realized that I could never do it in my own power. **I had to overcome in the strength only God could provide through Christ Jesus!**

I confessed to God my utter dependence on His power to not only save, but also to deliver. This is a scriptural principle. James 4:10 reads, *Humble yourselves in the sight of the Lord, and he shall lift you up.* 1 Peter 5:5-6 teaches, *God resisteth the proud, and giveth grace to the humble. Humble yourselves therefore under the mighty hand of God, that he may exalt you in due time.* You see, God wants us to humble ourselves, admit we need His help, and give our lives to Him to control.

I have found that there are steps of action in the humbling process. As we grow in the Lord, God will reveal various areas of our life that need to be given over to Him. As we continue to surrender, He will continue to lift us up. If we do the humbling, He will do the exalting. They work hand-in-hand. It's impossible to have one without the other. My dear friend, if you will humble yourself in your efforts to overcome your habits in your own power and realize you are powerless without God's help through Christ Jesus, the Scriptures will prove to be true. God will exalt you and lift you out of your addictive lifestyle! Then, and only then, will you be able to stand with Him against those things that seek to destroy you.

SUPPORT OF BAD FRIENDS

A second way that society will try to lead us to freedom is through the support of bad friends. Leaning on our friends as our way to freedom can often lead us away from God. They may have our best interest at heart; but if they are not guided by the Lord Jesus Christ, they will be unable to lead us to freedom. Second Corinthians 6:14 says, *Be ye not unequally yoked together with unbelievers: for what fellowship hath righteousness with unrighteousness? And what communion hath light with darkness?* We will explain these verses in detail in a later chapter, but for now I ask you to realize this truth: those living in darkness cannot help us get to the light.

Psalm 1:1 and 6 says, *Blessed is the man that walketh not in the counsel of the ungodly, nor standeth in the way of sinners, nor sitteth in the seat of the scornful. For the LORD knoweth the way of the righteous: but the way of the ungodly shall perish.* According to this verse, if we get advice from bad people, or hang out with bad people, or act like bad people, we will be unhappy and perish. You can follow their leading if you want, but you will not appreciate where it will take you.

Remember, *your recovery depends on following Jesus as your Way out of addiction* – period.

GOVERNMENT SOCIAL PROGRAMS

A third way to freedom taught by society is through governmental social programs. This way teaches that the path to freedom is wide and all-inclusive. There are no restrictions on this path. We can bring other habits (cigarettes, foul language, sexual immorality, etc.) with us as we overcome the ones we don't like.

Nothing could be further from the truth. No real freedom will ever be consistently experienced if we choose to feed one addiction or habit while attempting to starve another. Ephesians 4:22-24 teaches that we are to ...*put off concerning the former conversation* [or, lifestyle] *the old man, which is corrupt according to the deceitful lusts; and be renewed in the spirit of your mind; and that ye put on the new man, which after God is created in righteousness* [or, right living] *and true holiness* [or, set apart from worldly ways].

I've been to so many programs in an attempt to overcome my various addictions. I was often encouraged to overlook my smoking habits and sexual cravings while attempting to find freedom in "more important" areas. As a result, I would smoke as many cigarettes as I could! The language in those meetings was so dirty that even though I was living in sin, I felt like I needed to take a shower from the filth of the language in the room! The constantly critical spirits toward authority and nonstop talking about drinking only left me thirsty!

Why is it that we are willing to abort one unwanted addiction only to end up feeding another unwanted one? It's because we believe the lie that the path to freedom from our bad habits is wide and all inclusive with no restrictions on other sins.

However, according to our key verse--John 14:6--there is only one way to freedom. That way is not found in our power, our friends, our pride, or our "sin swapping." This "way" is found in God's Son, Jesus!

JESUS IS THE ONLY WAY

Our key verse (John 14:6) tells us, *Jesus saith unto him, I am the way...* "The" means *the only* way! There is no other way that works.

In Matthew 7:13 Jesus also said, *Enter ye in at the strait gate:* (He then begins to describe a gate other than that strait gate. He describes the gate that most people walk through.) *for wide is the gate, and broad is the way, that leadeth to destruction, and many there be which go in thereat.* Did you catch that? Wide is the gate, and broad is the way [many are the ways] that leads to destruction!

Ask yourself these questions.
- Through which gate am I attempting to find freedom?
- Which path am I on?
- Is it a wide gate?
- Is it a broad way?
- Will it lead to destruction?
- Are there many going through that gate?
- Have many others gone this way before me and failed?

If you have answered "yes" to those questions, you need to change your path from the way of the world to the way of God's Son.

After Jesus described the wide gate and broad path that leads many to destruction, He described that strait gate in verse 14. *Because strait is the gate, and narrow is the way, which leadeth unto life, and few there be that find it.*

Few there be that find it? Why would the narrow way which leads to freedom from the devil's bondage have the sad description of "few there be that find it?" Because the strait gate is Jesus. His gate is not all-inclusive. Everyone is welcome, but many reject this way because it is not dependent on our work. It is completely dependent on the Lord Jesus Christ. It is narrow because there are few people who will give up on their self-effort and lean on Jesus. They fail to believe in Him alone to save and change them. Therefore, they fail to find freedom. Jesus is the Only Way, and ...*no man cometh unto the Father, but by* [Him].

How has God shown He is for us? Through Christ Jesus, the Way! To help us understand this principle, we are going to use a parable [a story with a truth to be understood] given in John 10:1-10.

Throughout this passage, I will dissect and define Bible words. This will help us understand the truths that the Lord intends for us to understand:

> *Verily, verily, I say unto you, He that entereth not by the door into the sheepfold, but climbeth up some other way, the same is a thief, and a robber.* [In other words, there is a sheepfold. It has a door in which you enter. If you try to enter any other way, you are considered a thief and a robber.] *But he that entereth in by the door is the shepherd of the sheep ...and the sheep follow him: for they know his voice. And a stranger will they not follow, but will flee from him: for they know not the voice of strangers. This parable* [a story with a truth to be understood] *spake Jesus unto them: but they understood not. Then said Jesus ...I am the door of the sheep. All that ever come before me are thieves and robbers* [those who came before must have tried to enter some other way to be considered thieves and robbers, as mentioned earlier in the verse] *but the sheep did not hear them. I am the door: by me* [by the door of Jesus] *if any man enter in, he shall be saved* [First saved, then...] *and find pasture* [fulfillment in life; that's freedom in Christ]. *The thief* [the person who boasts of some other way] *cometh not but for to steal, and to kill, and to destroy* [That sounds like the destructive nature of our addictions].

If today you are struggling with a stubborn habit or addiction, what do these verses mean to you? It's very simple. The straight and narrow gate spoken of in Matthew 7:13-14 is the same door spoken of in this passage: it is Jesus Christ. Now, do you want to enjoy this way of pasture called freedom? It is an absolute freedom from not only the penalty of sin, but from the power of stubborn habits and addiction as well! To receive this freedom, you must enter through that narrow gate of Jesus. He is the only way to freedom!

Now who is this thief? The thief is that which tries to convince us that we can find freedom some other way rather than the door. In other words, society's many paths to freedom have been our thief. They have stolen our joy, killed our potential, and destroyed our life. They have robbed us of <u>a happiness that most people don't even know is possible!</u>

I'm sure by now you may be thinking, "Is it impossible for a person to overcome an addiction through programs in society?" I am sure there are people in society's programs that have overcome various habits and addictions. Yet, I am equally sure that those people have had to put forth an incredible effort of self-discipline. They had to do all the work themselves. And I am sure that it appears to pay off. However – make no mistake about it – they are *not* truly free from the power of that sin. Every day that battle will be with them. They will spend most days fighting that desire on a daily basis, never truly being free.

It would be much like being a slave that has been set free by his master, yet chooses to wear his chains the rest of his life. Sure, he could find another profession and not belong to that master—but he wouldn't be truly free because he would still be bound by what had previously controlled him.

Jesus is the gate that leads to a life of freedom from the bondage of habitual sin, and you have found it (Matthew 7:13-14)! The devil is going to be after you, but don't get discouraged. This path is the only way to freedom. God's Word will be your navigational tool to keep you on the right path. Scripture lets us know right and wrong, so we know when to stand against those things God is against.

Personally, I've never been so free in my whole life! It's because I went through the right door after spending years trying to enter in so many different ways. I have no shackles to weigh me down; I'm free! If you get on the one right way, you too will find freedom and live an abundant Christian life (John 10:10)!

Jesus, the Truth

Entering in at the right gate and realizing that Jesus is the way is just the beginning. Jesus also reminds us He is the truth. Once again, take note of our key verse, John 14:6: *I am the way, the truth, and the life; no man cometh unto the Father but by me.*

The world teaches that there are many different truths that we can believe. But that can't be true! Truth will never conflict with itself. There must be one standard of truth whereby all else is judged. Our key verse tells us that the truth is Jesus Christ. So, how do we discern between what is truth and what is a lie? John 17:17 says God will *...sanctify [us]* [or set us apart] *through thy truth: thy word is truth.* We are supposed to discern right from wrong by using the Word of Truth, the Bible. Hebrews 4:12 says that *the word of God... is a discerner of the thoughts and intents of the heart.* It will tell us if our thoughts are right or wrong. Again, God's Word sets our standards so we can boldly say, "If God's against it, then so am I!"

Let's look at some of the lies of society. We will then analyze what our "standard of Truth," God's Word, has to say about these lies.

HOW WE LIVE WILL NOT AFFECT OUR RELATIONSHIP WITH A LOVING GOD.

The first lie of society is the false assumption that how we live our lives will not affect our relationship with a loving God. The general philosophy in society's programs is that we need to learn to discipline ourselves in that area of particular weakness, and the other "not-so-bad" areas have no real affect on our shortcomings. But according to 1 John 1:6, *If we say that we have fellowship* [partnership] *with* [God], *and walk in darkness* [spiritual blindness], *we lie, and do not the truth.* But on the other end of the spectrum, the very next verse says, *But if we walk in the light* [spiritual direction], *as he is in the light* (or, spiritual direction), *we have fellowship one with another, and the blood of Jesus Christ his Son cleanseth us from all sin* [(or, our wrongdoings].

In other words, **we cannot reject truths of God's Word and say we are in a right relationship with God.** It doesn't work. Sin always breaks fellowship! However, if we seek spiritual direction and deal with areas of sin as God directs us, fellowship is restored and we will walk in a right relationship with Him.

For many years I believed this lie of society. I knew that I had a problem with drinking and with drug addiction. However, I thought if I was able to overcome those two areas of my life, I would be a good person. But that is far from being true. I had deep-seeded sins that were embedded in my heart. I overlooked these sins, refusing to surrender them to the Lord. As these seeds of sin grew, they eventually led to my alcoholism and drug addiction. By focusing on my addiction while overlooking its root cause, I was walking in a lie. The truth was that I had failed to walk in fellowship with God. I was walking in my own power, not in the truth of Christ Jesus. My fellowship with God was only going to be restored by walking in the light of spiritual direction found in God's Word. This spiritual direction reveals our heart's sin. As we confess and forsake that sin, our relationship with God is restored.

THERE IS NO RIGHT FROM WRONG.

A second lie of society is that there is no right from wrong. There was a time in my life (though not a very long period of time) that I thought my lifestyle was not wrong. I was in my early twenties, holding a job, and social drinking, but I wasn't really living a bad life. I was enjoying myself, and I convinced myself that there was nothing wrong with my style of entertainment. I was just so sure that it was not sin.

The world teaches us that there is nothing wrong with certain sins: social drinking, smoking, bad music, casual sex… the list could go on. But 1 John 1:8 and 10 says, *If we say that we have no sin, we deceive ourselves, and the truth is not in us. If we say that we have not sinned, we make him a liar, and his word is not in us.*

The remedy for our sin is laid out in 1 John 1:9. *If we confess* [agree with God about] *our sins* [wrongdoings], *he is faithful* [consistent] *and just* [right] *to forgive* [cease to hold to our charge] *us our sins* [wrongdoings], *and to cleanse us* [make us feel better] *from all unrighteousness* [sinful behavior].

SOME CAN CLAIM TO BE CHRISTIAN, YET THEIR LIFESTYLE WILL SHOW OTHERWISE.

A third lie of society is that some can claim to be Christian, yet their lifestyle will show otherwise. 1 John 2:4 says, *He that saith, I know him* [Jesus], *and keepeth not his commandments is a liar, and the truth is not in him.* Once again, we are focusing on what the Bible says is truth and what the Bible says is a lie. According to this verse, if you say you know Jesus Christ, but yet you don't obey his commandments, you are a liar and the truth [Jesus] is not in you.

If we never grow in our Christian life, or never experience any God-given victory over sin, or if we are unable or unwilling to obey biblical commandments that especially deal with our wrongdoings, it could be that the Truth is not in us! First John 2:3, 5-6 go on to say,

> *And hereby we do know that we know him* [here is how we know if we are a child of God], *if we keep* [obey] *his commandments. But whoso keepeth his word, in him verily is the love of God perfected: hereby know we that we are in him. He that saith he abideth in him* [Jesus] *ought himself also so to walk, even as he* [Jesus] *walked.*

It is not a power in us to obey, but rather a submission to God's power that produces obedience. *In Him* means "to be under His control". If we are in Him, we will keep His Word.

As you begin growing in your Christian life, gaining victory over various habits, developing godly friendships, and serving in your local church, please remember this: there will be other people in society and in churches who will claim to be Christians, but their lifestyle will show otherwise. They have missed an important point of Christian faith: **God has shown He is for us through Christ Jesus, so we can show we are His by taking a stand against the things He is against.**

Inconsistent lifestyles can tempt us to give ground to the enemy that we have already reclaimed for the cause of Christ. It is a lie of the world that God doesn't expect obedience from his children. If we abide in Him, we ought to walk as Jesus walked.

Though perfection will never be achieved here on earth, we ought to always be growing. Jesus, who was perfect, had to grow in wisdom as a child. As a new child of God, He stimulates growth through victory over revealed sin. When we gain victory, we experience spiritual growth. That's how we can be sure the Truth, Jesus, is in us.

JESUS WAS A GREAT MAN, BUT HE WAS NOT THE CHRIST, OUR ATONING ONE.

A fourth lie of society is that Jesus was a great man, maybe even a prophet. But He was not the Christ, our Atoning One. First John 2:22 says, *Who is a liar but he that denieth that Jesus is the Christ? He is antichrist that denieth the Father and the Son.* According to this verse, whoever says that Jesus Christ is anything less than the Savior of the world is a liar. The truth is found in John 3:16: *For God so loved the world, that he gave his only begotten Son* [Jesus], *that whosoever believeth in him* [Jesus] *should not perish, but have everlasting life.* We serve a risen Savior!

Jesus, the Son of God, came to earth as a propitiation [payment] for our sins. Because of His perfection and personal freedom from the law of sin and death, He is the only One that can truly set us free from the penalty and power of sin! He paid the debt that we could not pay. Our sin demanded our lives, resulting in an eternity in hell. But His blood was shed for our sake. We need only to accept His payment as our own! Whether we accept it or not, the payment is made. Man's part is only to believe and receive.

CHRISTIANS ARE HYPOCRITES WHO SHOW A LACK OF COMPASSION FOR OTHERS.

A fifth lie of society is that Christians are hypocrites who show a lack of compassion, even a hatred for others–including other Christians. Let's look at two passages out of 1 John.

- 1 John 3:15: *Whosoever hateth his brother is a murderer...*
- 1 John 4:19-20: *We love [Jesus], because he first loved us. If a man say, I love God, and hateth his brother, he is a liar: for he that loveth not his brother whom he hath seen, how can he love God whom he hath not seen?*

These verses are saying that an outward evidence of an inward relationship with God is a compassion for others, especially for other children of God. God's children should never be apathetic to the needs and faults of others. It is sad that in some churches we see a lot of inner bickering, criticism, and negativity when discussing needy Christians. This doesn't please God! That type of behavior is of one who is a liar and does not love God.

When I used to attend various addiction programs in society, people would testify of their "higher power" being the primary reason why they were able to overcome their addiction. I didn't really feel as if I had a higher power. I thought I loved God, but I didn't have a strong relationship with Jesus Christ. However, as my relationship with Christ grew, I wanted to proclaim His name and let everyone know of the victory that He had given to me. I would go to these various programs and ecstatically testify that my higher power was Jesus Christ. The room would get very quiet. At times, I would be asked not to speak in detail concerning my particular higher power and His identity. It was as if these so-called "brothers" hated me or my higher power! Maybe they did! The reason Jesus Christ is somewhat offensive to them is because they had fallen for the previously discussed lie that Jesus was just a good man.

If you are in such a program, let me remind you that how they react to and talk about Christians should be an underlying factor in your decision whether you should stay under their personal counsel. As discussed previously, our training should come from someone who is seeking advice from God. If they are criticizing Christians and showing a lack of compassion for others, the Bible says that they are liars. The Truth [Jesus] is not in them.

God's truth is found in 1 John 4:21, 3:11 and 14:

> *And this commandment have we from him, that he who loveth God love his brother also... For this is the message that ye heard from the beginning, that we should love one another... We know that we have passed from death unto life, because we love the brethren. He that loveth not his brother abideth in death.* (emphasis added)

I have taken a few things that I remember as being lies in society's programs and compared them to the truths I have since found in God's Word. I know that good has come from these programs. The purpose of discussing these lies of society is not to criticize other programs. It is to analyze the truth. My main concern is for the eternal destiny of your soul, not your current battle with addiction! God can take your addiction away in but a moment, but hell lasts forever! There is a better way than those society offers and that is God's Truth – His Son, Jesus!

Now, I want to show you where all of these lies in society are coming from. They are not coming from the well-meaning people who are feeding them to you. They are coming from the devil himself.

Who makes a truth or a lie? There's a father for each – an origin, if you will. The devil is the father of all lies; and he has an intention for each one of those lies. His purpose is to keep us in the dark, to keep us from getting saved. And if we are already saved, his purpose is to keep us from growing in the grace of God and knowledge of Jesus Christ. Once we receive Christ as our personal Savior, the devil can never get control of our eternal destiny. We are children of God for all time. However, if he can keep our testimony [the story of our life] from affecting other people's lives, he then succeeds in making us useless Christians.

John 8:44 says, *Ye are of your father the devil, and the lust of your father ye will do.* [Now he describes the devil.] *He was a murderer from the beginning and abode not in the truth, because there is* no truth in him. *When he speaketh a lie, he speaketh of his own: for he is a liar and* the father of it. The devil is the father of all lies. If the devil is the father of all lies, then it is equally easy to discover the origin of all truth. Let's see what the Bible teaches us about the Father of Truth.

Look again at our key verse, John 14:6: *Jesus* [God's Son] *saith unto him, I am the way, the truth, and the life: no man cometh unto the Father, but by me.* We have already settled that Jesus is the Truth. If Jesus is Truth, and God is His Father (both physically and spiritually), that makes God the Father of the Truth. The devil is the father of all lies, and God is the Father of all Truth. God created what is right; the devil created what is wrong. These two facts are the basis for the battle within each of us. Who will control you? Right or wrong? Truth or lies? God, or the devil?

Thus, we can conclude that the Truth, Jesus, is our source of freedom from all sin. To fully comprehend this principle, let's look at John 8:31-32. These verses contain a formula for freedom. I believe that these two verses are the two most important verses in the Word of God on how to find freedom from the penalty and power of sin and its habitual hold on people! By dissecting and defining this verse, let's discover Christ's formula for freedom.

FORMULA FOR FREEDOM

> *Then said Jesus to those Jews which believed on him, If ye continue in my word, then are ye my disciples indeed; and ye shall know the truth, and the truth shall make you free. (John 8:31-32)*

Step #1 of our formula for freedom is to **believe on Jesus** *(Then said Jesus to those Jews which believed on him…)*. The very first key to being set free from our addiction, from the power and penalty of sin, and from the control the devil has on us is to believe on Jesus!

- Mark 9:23: *Jesus said unto him, if thou canst believe, all things are possible to him that believeth.*
- John 3:16b: *Whosoever believeth in him should not perish, but have everlasting life.*

If you have not taken this first step, then stop taking your twelve steps! They are a waste of time! Step #1 is to believe on Jesus.

Step #2 of our formula for freedom is to **continue in His Word** *(If ye continue in my word)*. Jesus' Word is the Bible. John 15:7 says, *If ye abide in me, and my word abide in you, ye shall ask what ye will, and it shall be done unto you.* So many of us have gone to the Lord in prayer and said, "Oh, Lord, will You please remove this addiction, this stubborn habit, that I have? Could You please find it in Your heart, Lord, to help me?" But the Bible says that God's Word must abide in us to have our prayers answered. God will answer that prayer, but it requires that the Word of God abide in us.

God's Word cannot abide in us if we are not spending time in the Word of God. It's so easy to allow it to become a low priority in our lives. We will read for a period of time, then we go a few days without reading. The key is to *continue* in His Word. The fruit of daily persistence in reading, studying, memorizing, and meditation on the Bible will produce spiritual freedom. Our addictions and stubborn habits will eventually be overcome as God's Word abides in us and we abide in Him. This means that God's Word goes in and we yield to it. That is His Word abiding **in you** and you **in Him**. That brings victory!

Second Timothy 3:14-17 says,

> *But continue thou in the things which thou hast learned and hast been assured of, knowing of whom thou hast learned them. And that from a child thou hast known the holy scriptures, which are able to make thee wise unto salvation through faith which is in Christ Jesus. All scripture is given by inspiration of God, and is profitable* [the Bible's main purpose is] *for doctrine* [what is right], *for reproof* [what is not right], *for correction* [how to get right], *for instruction in righteousness* [how to stay right]: *that the man of God may be perfect, thoroughly furnished unto all good works.*

If we put those definitions together, we see that the main purpose for the Word of God is to teach a Christian what is right, what is not right [truth and lies], how to get right and how to stay right. It teaches us to stand for those things God is for, and against those things He is against. Why does the Lord want to teach us what's right, what's not right, how to get right, and how to stay right? So ...*that the man of God* [the Christian] *may be perfect, thoroughly furnished* [equipped] *unto all good works.*

Step #3 of our formula for freedom is to **be His disciple** (*Then are ye my disciples indeed* [John 8:31]). A disciple is a student who follows his leader. This means that as we study under Jesus, we must also follow Him with our lives. Matthew 16:24-25 says, *Then said Jesus unto his disciples, If any man will come after me, let him deny himself, and take up his cross, and follow me. For whosoever will save his life shall lose it: and whosoever will lose his life for my sake shall find it.* The cross that Jesus carried to Calvary and was hung upon was not His cross to bear; it was ours. He died for us! He died for you!

He died in our place! That cross belonged to us. The cross was our burden to carry - not Jesus'; and He bore that burden for us. Matthew 16:24-25 is teaching us that if we want to follow Jesus, we must deny our own desires and pick up someone else's burdens. Pick up someone else's problems and carry them on our shoulders. We need to die to ourselves and follow Jesus' perfect example of meeting the needs of a dying world!

For whosoever will save his life shall lose it. We like to focus on our own problems and our prosperity. But if we do, we will lose it all. But *...whosoever will lose his life for my sake shall find it.* Give your life to serve Jesus and you will find a life worth living, free from sin's power.

Step #4 of our John 8:32 formula for freedom is that we will know Truth (*And ye shall know the Truth...*). Second Peter 3:18 says, *But grow in grace, and in the knowledge of our Lord and Saviour Jesus Christ.* That is the goal of a disciple or student follower of Jesus. The more we get to know Jesus, the greater our level of freedom! John 8:32 tells us the result of our belief in Jesus and remaining under the influence of the Word: *...and the truth* [Jesus] *shall make you free.* A new child of God won't know Jesus very well. However, the more we get to know Jesus, the more we will learn about Him and His freedom!

Let's dissect and define Hebrews 5:13-14 to understand the growth process of a new Christian.

> *For every one that useth milk* [the simple things in the Bible] *is unskillful in the word of righteousness* [right living]: *for he is a babe* [new Christian]. *But strong meat belongeth to them that are of full age* [grown up], *even those who by reason of use* [repeated experiences] *have their senses* [thought processes] *exercised* [trained] *to discern* [consider] *both good and evil.*

This verse is teaching us that when we first come to Christ, we won't understand everything in the Bible. But don't get discouraged about that! God will help us understand little bits and pieces as we continue to learn the Bible. So when you study the Bible, be patient with yourself! Be willing to learn a little at a time. The Lord is giving you just a little bit of "milk" because you are just a little baby. If He gave you strong truths, it would ruin your digestive system and stunt your spiritual growth!

Think about it this way. If we were to feed a baby a steak, it would destroy his digestive system. He just isn't ready for the "strong meat" yet. Likewise, when the Bible feeds us milk, we grow spiritually and become strong. Then we can begin taking in strong meat as we develop. Strong meat is for those who are ...*of full age, even those who by reason of use have their senses exercised to discern both good and evil.* This means that they have used the Bible so much to discern what's right [doctrine], what's not right [reproof], how to get right [correction], and how to stay right [instruction in righteousness], that their thoughts are trained to consider both good and evil. They can continue in the Word because the Word continues in them. They know how to stand in His strength against those things God is against.

All freedom is found in knowing Jesus and having a personal relationship with Him. *Through Christ Jesus, God is for us.* That relationship comes from believing in Him and a willingness to be His student follower under the textbook of the Bible.

These four steps added together equal freedom. ...*And the Truth* [Jesus] *shall make you free* (John 8:32b) Can you see how it all ties together? The more we know Jesus, the more freedom we gain! This takes the "us" right out of it. **We're not the ones who make ourselves free.** We are unable to do it. It's Jesus Christ alone that allows us to experience any kind of freedom, and it's only through His prerequisites of belief and discipleship.

Remaining free from our addictions will require our yielding to His Spirit. That's where "continuing in His Word" comes in. You see, we have a free will and a choice to return to this bondage. It's as if the prison doors are open and we choose to remain inside. Or, we come out of the prison doors, only to return when under pressure. We have a choice. Proverbs 26:11 says, *As a dog returneth to his vomit, so a fool returneth to his folly.* We are free. It is up to us to respond properly to our release from sin's custody and control!

If we stay busy serving the Lord and being His disciple [student follower], it will help us avoid temptation. Romans 6:18 says, *Being then made free from sin, ye became the servants of righteousness.* Because He's made us free, it is our duty to become a servant of righteousness. If we decide to use this freedom as opportunity to live our own life, we will fail. There's no option about it. His desire is that we serve Him because of what He has done for us. Service to others is an evidence of our appreciation for our salvation!

Finally, we need to remain unmovable in our beliefs. Galatians 5:1 says, *Stand fast* [unmovable] *therefore in the liberty* [freedom] *wherewith Christ hath made us free, and be not entangled again with the yoke of bondage.* Without exception, we have to be for the things God is for and against the things He is against.

Jesus is the Truth. The more we know of Jesus the more freedom we will gain. And, friend, *If the Son therefore shall make you free, you shall be free indeed* (John 8:38)!

Jesus, the Life

We are only afforded one life while here on earth. We all want a full and enjoyable life, but how do we attain that? And how do we gain this type of life while at the same time overcoming sin? Let's look at some of the world's philosophy on what makes a good life and compare it to Jesus, who is "the life."

THE ACCRUAL OF EARTHLY POSSESSIONS DEMONSTRATES A SUCCESSFUL LIFE.

While addicted to drugs, I realized that by dealing narcotics I could acquire many worldly possessions. I foolishly believed that once I received those possessions, I'd be a happy man. That definitely proved to be a lie! Society will tell us that the accrual of earthly possessions demonstrates a successful life. But what does Jesus say?

Luke 12:15 says, *And he* [Jesus] *said unto them, Take heed; and beware of covetousness* [the desire to have things that other people have] *for a man's life consisteth not in the abundance of the things which he possesseth.* I am so grateful that I discovered this truth! I'm not against having nice things, and God isn't either. However, we err when our life is focused on the **abundance** of possessions. Life consists of so much more than the abundance of the things that we possess. God has promised to meet our needs, but only if our life is focused on *His* heavenly possessions. Philippians 4:19 says, *But my God shall supply all your need according to his riches in glory by Christ Jesus.*

The Bible gives a parable [a story that tells of a lesson to be learned] of a rich man who made the mistake of believing that a successful life was dependent on his accrual of earthly possessions and enjoyable entertainment. Let us learn from his mistake.

> *And he* [Jesus] *spake a parable unto them, saying, The ground of a certain rich man brought forth plentifully: And he thought within himself saying, What shall I do, because I have no room where to bestow my fruits? And he said, This will I do: I will pull down my barns, and build greater; and there will I bestow all my fruits and my goods. And I will say to my soul, Soul, thou hast much goods laid up for many years; take thine ease, eat, drink, and be merry. But God said unto him, Thou fool, this night thy soul shall be required of thee: then whose shall those things be, which thou hast provided? So is he that layeth up treasure for himself, and is not rich toward God. And he* [Jesus] *said unto his disciples, Therefore, I say unto you, Take no thought for your life, what ye shall eat;*

neither for the body, what ye shall put on. The life is
more than meat, and the body is more than raiment.
(Luke 12:16-23)

This rich man in Luke 12 had a bumper crop. He decided to build bigger and better barns for his abundant harvest. He was set for many years to come; life was good! What did he do then? He decided to just take life easy, to eat, drink, and be merry. Oh, how foolish! That night his life was required of him. He was a man who had been blessed, had more than he would ever need. But instead of focusing on how he could use his abundance for the Lord's work, or how he could better serve others; he decided to pool all that money into earthly possessions and to enjoy his life. He died that night, probably from drunkenness!

There is a moral to this story that will help us avoid this catastrophe in our life: **Love God rather than life.** This will result in a true and God-honoring love of life. In this life, many are searching for happiness. All the years I struggled with my addiction, I was looking for love, enjoyment, happiness, contentment, and financial prosperity. These were the things that the Lord kept from me! Since my change of focus from self toward God, I have found a true joy and contentment in my life that only God could give. It is a joy and contentment that without Him, man could never attain.

To help us better understand this, let's dissect and define 1 John 2:15-17:

> *Love not the world, neither the things that are*
> *in the world. If any man love the world, the love of*
> *the Father is not in him. For all that is in the world,*
> *the lust of the flesh, and the lust of the eyes, and the*
> *pride of life, is not of the Father, but is of the world.*
> *And the world passeth away, and the lust thereof: but*
> *he that doeth the will of God abideth for ever.*

Love not the world. What is the "world?" God gives us a definition in the very next verse: *For all that is in the world,* [first] *the lust of
the flesh;* [second] *the lust of the eyes, and* [third], *the pride of life.* The
world is made up of the lust of the flesh, the lust of the eyes, and the
pride of life. You are probably asking right now, "What in the world
does that mean?" Let's look at each one.

The lust of the flesh is a controlling desire to do. The lust of
the flesh is the controlling desire that tempts you to do anything you
could ever want to do. If a man could do anything he ever wanted
to do in his lifetime no matter what it was... go to a Chicago Bears
game, fly the fastest jet around the world, talk with the president, go
to Disneyland, anything he ever wanted to do... that would be a man
who has gained one-third of the world. However, there's still two-
thirds of the world yet to gain.

The lust of the eyes is a compulsive urge to have. What you
see, you want. If a man could *have* anything he ever wanted during
his lifetime... a new car, nice big house, his very own island, his own
country, anything he ever wanted... that would be a man who has
gained the second third of the world. But there is still one-third left.

The pride of life is the consuming urge to be. The pride of life
is what you want to become: "If I could be the president of my high
school class... if I could be the president of a corporation... if I could
be the President of the United States... if I could be a dictator of the
world..." If a man could *be* whatever he ever wanted to be during
his lifetime, this would be a man who has gained the last third of
the world.

So, if a man could *do* anything he ever wanted to do, *have*
anything he ever wanted to have, or *be* anything he ever wanted to
be during his lifetime, this would be a man who would have gained
the entire world! However, the Bible says that if you were to take that
man who could *do, have,* or *be* it all and set him on one end of a scale
with a new convert crippled with addiction on the other end of the
scale, and ask the Lord to choose which one is of more value to him,
He will choose the person with the addiction, the person crippled

with the sin. Why? Because the addict crippled by sin is more likely to receive God's offer of life through Jesus Christ than to lean on himself. Therefore, the addict is more likely to live a life that shows what God is for and against.

Matthew 16:26 says, *For what is a man profited, if he shall gain the whole world, and lose his own soul?* What does it profit a man if he gains everything he ever wanted to do, be, or have, yet he loses his own soul? The verse in 1 John goes on to explain why it is futile to gain the whole world: *the world passeth away, and the lust* [the desires to do, be, and have] *thereof: but he that doeth the will of God abideth for ever.*

At the conclusion of the parable of the rich man, Luke 12:31 reminds us, *But rather seek ye <u>first</u> the kingdom of God, and all these things* (that you want to be, do, or have) *shall be added unto you.*

THERE IS ONLY ONE LIFE; LIVE IT UP!

"You only live life once, so just live it up!" But Jesus taught that our life should be sacrificed. When we do so, He can bless us with a better life. Once again, we see in Luke 17:33 that, *Whosoever shall seek to save his life shall lose it; and whosoever shall lose his life shall preserve it.* Proverbs 8:35 also tells us, *for whoso findeth me* [Jesus] *findeth life, and shall obtain favor of the Lord.*

There is an old saying that is so simple, but yet so true: "'Tis one life will soon be past. Only what's done for Christ will last." Jesus wants us to sacrifice this life for His cause. There may be only one life here in this world, but there is good news, my friend. This life can be better, and there is another life after this one.

Luke 18:29-30 says:

> *And he* [Jesus] *said unto them, Verily I say unto you, there is no man that hath left house, or parents, or brethren, or wife, or children, for the king- dom of God's sake* [in other words, there's nothing we wouldn't give up for God] *who shall not receive*

manifold more in this present time and in the world
to come life everlasting.

What a wonderful promise from God! There's nothing that we can give up, nothing that we can sacrifice, no matter what it is, that God will not give us much more in return in this life and in the life to come. He will not only give us more, but He will give us a life that lasts forever. Amen to that!

...Once to Die

Hebrews 9:27 says, *It is appointed unto men once to die, but after this the judgment.* Unfortunately, for those of us who are not focused on giving to the Lord our lives, God reminds us that this life will end in His judgment.

- Romans 14:10b *...for we shall all stand before the judgment seat of Christ.*
- 2 Corinthians 5:10 *For we must all appear before the judgment seat of Christ; that every one may receive the things done in his body, according to that he hath done, whether it be good or bad.*

Our entire lives we have heard lies about how we should live, for whom we should live, what is right and what is wrong, different ways to get to heaven... many lies, only one Truth. The Truth is free and obtainable through belief in God's Son, Jesus Christ. Remember God's plan?

- John 3:16: *For God so loved the world, that he gave his only begotten Son, that whosoever believeth in him should not perish, but have everlasting life.*
- Romans 10:9-10: *That if thou shalt confess with thy mouth the Lord Jesus, and shalt believe in thine heart that God hath raise*

him from the dead, thou shalt be saved. For with the heart man believeth unto righteousness; and with the mouth confession is made unto salvation.

Do you believe in your heart that God sent Jesus to die for your sins and three days later He rose from the grave, defeating death? You need only to accept Christ's payment of your sin debt by receiving His gift of eternal life. Faith in Jesus will save you from eternal life in hell and replace it with eternal life in heaven. First John 5:13 says, *These things have I written unto you that believe on the name of the Son of God; that ye may know that ye have eternal life and that ye may believe on the name of the Son of God.*

The Freedom to Draw the Line Comes from Whom Controls You

Freedom from addiction is not freedom from drugs and alcohol. It's not freedom from pornography; and it's not freedom from smoking, television, or the love of money. **Freedom from addiction is being out from under the control of this world and under the control of Jesus.** Freedom is control. It's not what controls you that separates freedom from bondage; it's **who** controls you that separates freedom from bondage. *Through Christ Jesus, God is for us!* That's God's honest Truth!

Throughout the Bible we see passages indicating behavior that God is against. He has asked that we avoid behaving in this way. He warns that participating in certain behavior will bring sorrow, punishment and can even lead to a shorter life. We have seen this to be true in not only our own lives, but in the lives of many others, as well. It is called the law of sowing and reaping. This simple law says if we sow [spread] destructive behavior, we will reap [receive] destruction in our life. But if we spread good behavior patterns, we will receive blessings from God.

We will focus on sowing, reaping, and drawing the line against the things God is against throughout this book. But for now, know this: **God is for us. The freedom He offers through Jesus Christ is proof.** And if we are to live in His freedom, we must accept Christ's offer for salvation first. Then we can draw the lines of behavior that pleases God and say, "If God is against it, so am I!"

Jesus is the only Way, the only Truth, and the only Life. Know Jesus and He will make you free... finally!

Every Sin Has Its Origin in Our Heart.

Let no man say when he is tempted, I am tempted of God: for God cannot be tempted with evil, neither tempteth he any man: But every man is tempted, when he is drawn away of his own lust, and enticed. Then when lust hath conceived, it bringeth forth sin: and sin, when it is finished, bringeth forth death

—James 1:13-15

When I first began my journey to end my addictions, I had a host of places and people to blame for my problems. Let me share just a few examples of how I placed that blame on anyone but myself.

- My close relatives destroyed my self-esteem when I was a child.
- The school bullies made fun of me on the playground.
- I didn't have enough material wealth growing up.
- I had too much material wealth growing up.
- My parents weren't expressive enough in telling me they loved me.
- My parents were too expressive when they told me they loved me.
- My teachers didn't help me feel smart enough.
- My coaches told me I was never big enough.

I could go on for a long time, but you get the idea. According to many "experts" I talked to, nothing was really my fault. My addiction had nothing to do with my choices. It was based on the "negative input" from everyone else. What a lie! The truth of the matter is, the problem *was* me. Where does sin begin, anyway? The answer is the principle for this chapter: **every sin has its origin in our hearts.**

Before I came to Christ, I tried to overcome my addictions over and over again through regular attendance to group meetings in society. I would spend hours upon hours sulking in my coffee, smoking cigarettes, and discussing my endless desire to drink.

Sound familiar? Why didn't this type of activity help me? Probably because instead of dealing with my sin as though I was responsible for it, I simply whined about it. Ephesians 5:11-12 reminds us to *have no fellowship with the unfruitful works of darkness, but rather reprove them. For it is a shame even to speak of those things which are done of them in secret.* Our sins of the past must be forgotten. To meditate upon them, and discuss them openly, only gives place to the devil. I decided a long time ago I would rather tell people what God has done for me than to tell people what I had done to God.

Constant meditation [thinking] on our desire to fulfill a fleshly lust will ultimately lead to acting out our desire. If we're fortunate to avoid it physically, we will seldom avoid it mentally. Proverbs 23:7 reads, *For as he thinketh in his heart, so is he.* Sin and good alike have their origins in our hearts.

For me to avoid the seemingly unending temptation to feed my addiction, I needed to discipline myself to avoid talking about it in a desirous way. I needed to avoid even thinking about it. By thinking about it, I was actually making it easy for myself to do wrong. Romans 13:14 states, *But put ye on the Lord Jesus Christ, and make not provision for the flesh, to fulfil the lusts thereof.*

I saw an old friend at a local grocery store. He had heard that I had stopped using drugs and had "found religion." I explained how Jesus had changed my life and given me power over my addictions to both drugs and alcohol. He exclaimed his gladness and went on to tell me that he had been sober for three weeks. He had finally quit his job that led to after-hours drinking and had moved out of his buddy's house (who liked to have drinking parties regularly). Realizing these were both good first steps, I encouraged him to visit church and offered to pick him up. He gave me his address.

Unfortunately, the young man had chosen to take up residence in an apartment that was directly adjacent to a popular bar in town. He never made it to church. Why did this man fail in his recovery? He made it easy for himself to do wrong. Even if he never left his house, the constant sounds of the music in the bar beneath him would never let the thought of drinking leave his mind!

You see, **the heart can accustom itself to sin or righteousness, depending upon the focus you choose.** An act that once would seem terrible and undeniably wrong can, by contemplating it too often, become attractive.

Proverbs 4:23 reads, *Keep thy heart with all diligence; for out of it are the issues of life.* Everything I ever searched for in life – the important issues of life: love, joy, peace, happiness, friendship, financial freedom – were always withheld from me during my times of addiction. Why was that? Because the important issues of life are given by God. He never entrusts them to those who do not work hard [diligently] to keep [guard] their hearts from being hardened from the deceitfulness of sin.

Where does sin begin? Remember, before you ever did it, you "thunk" it in your heart!

Belief Determines Behavior

Society tells us that **behavior determines belief.** If you behave a certain way, you are providing insight into your belief system: If you are a drinker, then you believe that drinking is acceptable behavior. If you smoke dope, then you believe there is nothing wrong with drug use. If you live immorally, then you do not believe in the importance of moral purity. If you criticize others, then you are showing that you believe there is nothing wrong with giving evil reports. This is the system of the world: behavior determines belief.

God, however, has created a different management system. His system teaches us that **belief should determine behavior.** In other words, what you hold in your heart is the source of the actions you take. For example, if a young woman of the night–a harlot, if you will–were to be introduced to a king and fell in love with him, you might think it an odd thing. And if that king subsequently fell in love with this harlot, you might think it even more odd. But if these two unlikely candidates for love were to marry and move into his royal castle, do you think she would continue her trade of prostitution when darkness falls upon the city streets? No way! She would find her former behavior detestable. Why? Because she is no longer a prostitute. She is a queen! She is the wife of a king. How perverse and profane it would be if she ever went back to living like a harlot! She is going to behave differently because she rightly believes she has changed. No longer is she a "business" woman; she is a lady of the highest order.

It is the same for you and for me. We have been adopted. We are children of the King of kings. That makes us royalty in His heavenly kingdom where Jesus is preparing a place for us. He has been working on it for over two thousand years. If He can create the splendor of the universe in six literal days, just think how marvelous our home in heaven must be by now. And because I *believe* this, I *behave* differently than I used to. You ought to as well.

Your identity is such that who you are in Christ determines how you behave. Often after conversion, new believers go from being ruled by the body of sin to trying to live righteously in their own power. The proper way to behave is predicated on understanding who you are in Christ – your new identity. You are His. He leads, you submit, and a supernatural power to face the circumstances of life is the guaranteed result. That is who we are in Christ.

It is as simple as follow the leader. We followed the devil before our conversion. Now we must resist the temptation to self-rule, which only leads us to fulfill the lusts of the flesh. Our "inner man" must overcome the "outer man" if we are to overcome sin. Our hearts must constantly be surrendered to God. They must become the source of obedient action. Spirit-rule is the key to the dynamic Christian walk in relation to God and others, as we will see.

The Two Commandments of Christ

Here are the two responsibilities upon which your freedom in Christ will hinge. If you will live with a conscious effort to obey these two responsibilities under the rule of the Holy Spirit, the first will remove your addiction, and the second will keep it from coming back: *Jesus said unto him, Thou shalt love the Lord thy God with all thy heart* [your emotions], *and with all thy soul* [your will], *and with all thy mind* [your thoughts]. *This is the first and great commandment* (Matthew 22:37-38).

LOVE THE LORD YOUR GOD

Our first responsibility is to God: to love *Him* with *all* our heart, with *all* our soul, and with *all* our mind. Our heart, soul, and mind are what I call our "outer man." It is who we are apart from God. The inner man, which is quickened [made alive] at salvation, is: where the Spirit of God lives. This is the part of our being that died in the Garden but was made alive upon the second birth. It is the part of us that communicates with God. The problem is that the outer man loves himself. Our love of self constrains the Spirit of God from flowing through us. The first and great commandment is telling us to love God with our outer man–our heart, soul, and mind. This is our responsibility to God. Meeting this responsibility will break the outer man, thus allowing the inner man to flow through us. **Meeting your responsibility to God will remove your addiction!** Let's look at each element of this responsibility.

All Your Heart

Our heart, if left uncorrected by God's Spirit, is the origin of sin against God. But it doesn't have to be that way. If we love God with all our heart, then we will love Him with our entire emotional being. The heart is the seat of emotions and passions. Emotional highs and emotional lows often lead to indulging in selfish sin, just as James 1:13-15 says. When we feel emotionally drained, we tend to get selfish. God's Spirit, who lives within us, cannot flow through us when our emotions are running or ruining our lives.

Sinful habits are often fueled by our unchecked emotions. But placing our emotions under the control of the Holy Spirit will allow God to defeat our outer man. Circumstances of life, which work together for our good, are allowed by God and are intended to break that outer man. Nevertheless, we get upset with these circumstances. We fail to see that God is working on our behalf through our circumstances. If we would look at these circumstances as being helpful to our development, then His joy – which is a fruit [outcome] of His Spirit – would flow through us even during adversity.

If you will learn to not yield to your emotions, you will love God with your entire heart. But there is more. You must love God with...

All Your Soul

The soul is the human will–what we want to do, what we want to be, what we want to have. Love God with *all* your soul. This requires a complete, sacrificial surrender of our will to exercise and experience life as we would prefer. We all have plans for our lives, both day-to-day and long-term. But do we consciously make these decisions in alignment with what we believe God would have us to do, be, or have?

What our souls want in life often conflicts with God's desires for our lives. We must force our desires [our human will] to yield to God's desires. We often think that if we were to get what we want out of life, it would bring contentment. When God gives us something different from what our souls desire, it is intended, once again, to work together for our good. Yet many times, we get frustrated with this; our wish is not His command. We follow after the flesh and allow God's ways truly to bother us. But God's ways are not our ways. *His will is intended to break our outer man so that the inner man can flow out of us. His will is to shape our will to accept His work in and around us, which aligns our hearts against sin.*

If you will accept this truth, you will begin to love God with all your soul, because your soul will love what God wants you to be, do, and have. Your outer man will be broken and God's Spirit will have free course. He will guide your every decision. Should you indulge in your addiction? That's a hard question for the soul to determine, at times, but it's an easy question for the one who is led by the Holy Spirit, rather than the soul. Love God with all your soul. Yet there is more. You must love God with...

All Your Mind

Loving God with all our mind is the most difficult of these three disciplines. Our mind, of course, is the center of our thought processes. The sins of the mind are, for the most part, private. I have found while counseling that when one loses a battle to sin, that battle began and was lost in the mind. *Every sin has its origin in our hearts, desires, and thoughts.* (Remember, we thought about it before we ever did it!)

Our minds need to be under the influence of the inner man, the Spirit of God. The hardest area of the outer man to control is the mind. It remains unpoliced. Our emotions can show, our desires can be measured by our actions, but the mind is everyone's secret hiding place.

We are not just discussing sins that would be readily considered wicked, such as sins of immoral or dishonest thinking. We can have a mind free of wicked thoughts and still have a mind that is under our control and not the control of God. Often times, what we see with Christians is a mixture of the inner man with the outer man in the area of our thoughts. We take a Spirit-led thought and mix it with our flesh. We mix God's prompting with our own points of advantage. If we are not careful, it is possible to think within ourselves that our decisions are Spirit-led. However, after an honest examination we find that they are mixed: God's leading stirred with man's preferences.

Hebrews 4:12 says, *For the word of God is quick, and powerful, and sharper than any two-edged sword, piercing even to the dividing asunder of soul and spirit, and of the joints and marrow, and is a discerner of the thoughts and intents of the heart.* Let's dissect and define this verse in terms of the inner man and outer man. I believe it will help us to hand over the real estate of our minds to God.

The writer of Hebrews is describing the Bible as being sharp – so sharp that it is sharper than a two-edged sword. A two-edged sword can cut to the bone, no matter which direction it is applied. This "sword" can pierce the joints (which are attached to the bone) and it can pierce the marrow (which is located within the bone). This tells us that the inside and the outside of a bone can be pierced by a two-edged sword. This illustration is a description of God's Word. It can pierce both the inner man [your spirit] and the outer man [your soul–mind, will, and emotions]. It goes on to say that the reason that this piercing is necessary is for ...*the dividing asunder* [apart] *of soul* [outer man] *and spirit* [inner man]! The verse then tells us that the Bible ...*is a discerner of the thoughts and intents of the heart.* We cannot discern our own hearts. Jeremiah 17:9 says that the heart is so wicked, we cannot even know it.

So what can we do to see to it that our mind is submitted to the mind of Christ? We must allow our soul and spirit to be separated by the Word of God, regularly, in our life's decisions. The Word of God will show us when our thoughts are not lining up with His thoughts, but only if we will apply the Sword to our mind–our outer man. 2 Corinthians 10:5c says we should be...*bringing into captivity every thought to the obedience of Christ.* Bring your thought process into captivity. Take your thoughts captive – with God holding the key!

As mentioned before, God allows circumstances in our lives to lead to the breaking of this stubborn, selfish outer man. The outer man wants to *feel* what he wants [emotions]. He wants to *do* what he wants [soul-will]. He wants to *think* what he wants [mind]. But if we will permit the circumstances God allows into our life to break the outer man, we will find that those wounds – which at one time were so hard to accept – are the very wounds that God will use to shine through to the world. Our shattered outer man obeys Christ, who dwells in our inner man. Our heart no longer gives birth to sin, but to righteousness in Christ.

When circumstances are not what you would choose for yourself, accept God's truth that ...*all things work together for good to them that love God, to them who are the called according to his purpose* (Romans 8:28). His purpose? The very next verse tells us what that is: ...*to be conformed to the image of his Son.* What image is that? The image of Jesus Christ–a Man who was tempted like us, but Whose outer man was submitted to His inner man, God's Spirit.

The key to the work of the Word in your life is the piercing and dividing of the soul [outer man] from the spirit [inner man]. God's Word intends to separate your soul [mind, will, and emotions] and your spirit [God in you]. Sometimes when God is giving us a leading, we begin to think about His direction. We begin to rationalize His will. Our emotions can begin to get involved and our stubborn wills react to His leading. Before we know it, our souls have cancelled out the Spirit's leading. We have taken God's thoughts or God's will or God's emotions and we have contaminated them with our selfish thoughts, desires, or feelings.

When we are making decisions apart from His Word, we may be deceived by our own judgment. But if we run to God's Word for our answers, He will separate our deceived hearts from His clear direction. The Bible will point out areas in our lives that need to be changed. God's Word is *a discerner of the thoughts and intents of the heart.* Your heart may not always tell you the truth, but the Word will.

What does it mean to be conformed to the image of Christ and to take on the mind of Christ? Philippians 2:5-8 defines what the mind of Christ was:

> *Let this mind be in you, which was also in Christ Jesus: Who, being in the form of God, thought it not robbery to be equal with God: But made himself of no reputation, and took upon him the form of a servant, and was made in the likeness of men: And being found in fashion as a man, he humbled himself, and became obedient unto death, even the death of the cross.*

I've heard it said before that the true test of a servant is if you act like one when you're being treated like one. If God is not treating you the way you want Him to, don't grumble. Do not complain. Do not let your thoughts run away with you. Accept your servant's role. You will then be conforming to His image by submitting to His mind, which is *in* you. Remember, you are not your own, so don't act as if you are. Give God the love of your mind. Let the Holy Spirit conform your heart to God's ways. If you will do this, He will make you a servant–a servant of others.

Choose to love God with your heart, soul, and mind. Your outer man will then be broken (as well as your stubborn habits and addictions), and you will be free to be led by your inner man [God's Spirit]. The inner man will lead you to others, and they are your second responsibility.

LOVE THY NEIGHBOR AS THYSELF

Jesus said our second responsibility is just like the first. *Love thy neighbor as thyself.* Our first responsibility is to God, and our second responsibility is to others. If our first responsibility of loving God will remove our addictions, then our second responsibility of loving others will keep our addictions from returning.

Sometimes this second responsibility seems more difficult than even the first. People are born selfish and self-centered. Every man since Adam was born with a dead spirit. When you were saved, that spirit came alive as the Holy Spirit came to dwell within you. Anything touched by God comes alive! Despite this glorious fact, we often find that we love ourselves very much. That's why our primary concern in life is for our *own* comforts, our *own* rights, what *we* want. But by shifting our focus off of ourselves and onto others, a specific change is inevitable. We will begin to see others as Jesus sees them. When this happens, it is a clear sign that God is shaping our hearts for His purposes – and that's right where we want to be.

God has clearly given the people within whom He dwells some *responsibilities to others.* His very purpose for dwelling within you is to flow through you and shine through your wounded and broken outer man. If we will accept these responsibilities as opportunities for Christ to shine, then the fruit of the Spirit will be evident in our lives. What a great life we can experience! It is the abundant Christian life!

Let's look at this responsibility to others as outlined in Romans 15:1-2 where we read, *We then that are strong* [capable] *ought* [are under obligation] *to bear the infirmities* [deterioration] *of the weak* [unstable], *and not to please ourselves. Let every one of us please his neighbour for his good to edification.* This does not mean you have to be a spiritual giant to meet this responsibility–just capable. If you are a Christian, then the capability lies within you. [You] *can do all things through Christ which strengtheneth* [you] (Philippians 4:13).

Dissected and defined, we are being commanded to bear the deterioration of unstable people. This is more important than pleasing ourselves. Our hearts must change to become a platform for God's work, and not the place where sin begins! Our selfish desire to please ourselves must go away. That doesn't mean that we are never able to be pleased. I think you will find that when you learn to focus on others, you learn to experience pleasure that you never thought possible.

When I began Reformers Unanimous, my wife and I decided to hold the weekly class on Fridays. We figured that if we could have a Bible study for addicts and keep them sober on Friday night with an invitation to return on Sunday, they might be able to find the power to stay sober on Saturday night. Then, after attending church on Sunday, they would return to work on Monday having remained abstinent from their addictions for the whole weekend. They would be happy and convince themselves to try it again the next week. It seemed like a great idea.

I convinced a friend to share the responsibility. I would run the class one Friday and he would run it the next. I devoted every other Friday to addicts. After about two months, my assistant stepped down, requiring me to teach every Friday. I had a choice to make: a bi-weekly Bible study that left its students vulnerable every other week, or forsake my own pleasures and give up every Friday night. I took the easy way out and left the decision up to my wife. I'm glad that I did. She chose to give up *every* Friday night from that point forward. Praise God, what a difference it has made!

Shortly after we made that commitment, our Bible study for a half-dozen addicts sprouted. Within a year it was up to thirty people and it doubled every year after that. Now our Rockford Reformers Unanimous reaches over three hundred addicts per week through the Bible study class and its local satellites. Since that time, that Bible study class model is now used in churches across America to reach the addicted. Each one is led by people who are making that very same sacrifice: exchanging self–pleasure for bearing the deterioration of unstable people. Who are the beneficiaries of these sacrifices? The addicts, yes. But these burden-bearers across America will tell you that it is *they* who have experienced the greater personal benefit. Such is true of all unselfish sacrifices. God rewards the sacrifice of your pleasures for the burden-bearing of the unstable with a freedom found only in Jesus.

Galatians 6:2 tells us, *Bear ye one another's burdens, and so fulfill the law of Christ*. We fulfill, or complete, the very teachings of Christ when we bear the burdens of others.

These are our two responsibilities: Love God with the outer man by yielding to the inner man, and love others by giving up our own pleasures for the benefit of those whose burdens are overbearing. If we will do this, we will experience the supernatural power of the Holy Spirit over the power of our addiction.

In fact, according to Jesus Himself, *on these two commandments hang all the Law and the Prophets* (Matthew 22:40). The Law and the Prophets are the summation of all the Old Testament biblical teachings, God's written Word at the time of Christ. The Ten Commandments (Exodus 20:1-20) would be considered the Law. As you read the Ten Commandments, notice how each one can be traced back to either our responsibility to God or our responsibility to others.

- **Commandments 1-4: Our Responsibility to God**
  Thou shalt have no other gods before me.
  Thou shalt not make unto thee any graven image.
  Thou shalt not take the name of the LORD thy God in vain.
  Remember the Sabbath day, to keep it holy.
- **Commandments 5-10: Our Responsibility to Others**
  Honour thy father and thy mother.
  Thou shalt not kill.

Thou shalt not commit adultery.
Thou shalt not steal.
Thou shalt not bear false witness against thy neighbor.
Thou shalt not covet....
Fear not: for God is come to prove you, and that his fear may be before your faces, that ye sin not.

We know that it is not possible to live our lives without breaking commandments. Yet the Law was not designed to *save* from sin, but to *convict* of sin. It is, and always has been, a valuable tool to discern the state of our hearts. Remember the Pharisees and Sadducees in the crowd that we spoke of earlier? They saw their salvation in the fulfilling of the Law. But the purpose of the Law is twofold: first, to purge sin out of our lives [*to prove you*] and, second, to keep sin from ruling our lives (*that his fear* [constant awareness of God's presence and my accountability to Him for my actions] *may be before your faces, that ye sin not*).

Notice the correlation between the twofold purpose of the Law and the Two Commandments of Christ: *Love the Lord thy God with all thy heart, and with all thy soul, and with all thy mind...* Meeting our first responsibility (to God) will remove our addiction, thus purging sin out of our life. *And the second is like unto it, Thou shalt love thy neighbor as thyself.* Meeting our second responsibility (to others) will help keep our addiction from returning, thus fulfilling the second purpose of the Law–keeping sin from ruling our life.

It is when our outer man begins to yield to these two commandments that we begin to experience the victorious Christian life! I guess it was put best when it was said that the key to experiencing JOY in our Christian life is when we yield to our responsibilities in this order: Jesus, Others, and then You. When those priorities are in place, they crowd out the desires in our hearts that so easily become sin.

We need not let our hearts be a place where sin originates. Instead, God can shape our hearts into places where our belief in Him generates behavior that honors Him.

It Is Easier to Keep the Heart Clean Than It Is to Clean the Heart After It Has Been Defiled.

I beseech you therefore, brethren, by the mercies of God, that ye present your bodies a living sacrifice, holy, acceptable unto God, which is your reasonable service. And be not conformed to this world: but be ye transformed by the renewing of your mind, that ye may prove what is that good, and acceptable, and perfect, will of God. —Romans 12:1-2

Keep thy heart with all diligence; for out of it are the issues [important things] of life.

Proverbs 4:23

When my wife and I were first married, I had quite a few lessons to learn. I was a 28-year-old bachelor and was not accustomed to cleaning up after myself. My favorite meal was Chili-n-Fries Surprise (the recipe is available for a small charge). My wife refused to cook it because of the extreme mess that the grease and chili sauce made on her white stove. I was forced to suffer. However, a friend of my wife's asked her to work a few hours every Monday afternoon at her beauty supply store. She consented, and I was left to fend for myself to obtain dinner on Monday nights. Praise the Lord, Chili-n-Fries Surprise!

In my desire to consume this long-awaited meal after I prepared it, I "overlooked" cleaning the stove. When the next Monday rolled around, I found the chili sauce and grease stains from the previous week's delicatessen still splattered on my wife's stove. It was gross.

There was no way I could prepare a meal on that filth. So when my wife arrived home later that evening, I asked her when she was planning to clean the stove. BIG MISTAKE. My careless comment launched us into our first fight.

I learned a valuable lesson that night. After an hour of scrubbing, I learned it is easier to keep a kitchen stove clean than to clean it after it has been stained. How much simpler would it have been to deal with the grease and mess of my Chili-n-Fries Surprise right away rather than to let it sit and form its own crust for a week?

The Bible teaches us this same truth: it's so much easier to keep the heart clean than to clean it after filth is layered over it. We can't afford to let a feel-good moment become the Chili-n-Fries that surprises us with how tough it is to clean up!

Over and over again in the Bible we are faced with examples of people who chose to associate with sin in hope that it would not lead them to a sinful condition. Think about Abraham's nephew Lot, for example. Lot was a righteous man (2 Pt. 2:8), yet he chose to associate with ungodly men (Psalm 1:1a). He had day-to-day contact with sin (Ps.1:1b). Morally, that sin was worse than the toughest grease a stove has ever seen. It defiled Lot's heart. He allowed the people around him to decay into moral wickedness with no good use for God (Ps. 1:1c). Yes, Lot's life was ultimately spared by God. However, he in no way prospered (Ps. 1:3). The last we hear of him, Lot was getting drunk and committing terrible sins (Gen. 19).

How can this mistake be avoided in your life? Follow these three simple verses:

- Proverbs 22:3: *A prudent man foreseeth the evil, and hideth himself: but the simple pass on, and are punished.* If you know something will defile you, pass it up!
- Proverbs 6:27-28: *Can a man take fire in his bosom, and his clothes not be burned? Can one go upon hot coals, and his feet not be burned?* In other words, there is no mystery about what things will defile your heart.
- Proverbs 4:23 *Keep thy heart with all diligence; for out of it are the issues* [important things] *of life.* "With all diligence" means "with every means possible." Do everything you can to keep you heart pure! Keep it clean in the first place!

Three Dedications to Keep Your Heart Undefiled

We have learned in order to live freely from this world of bondage that we must walk one way, believe one truth, and for one life – the way, truth, and life of our Lord Jesus Christ. That is God's plan for not only providing freedom from the penalty of sin, but His prerequisite for providing emancipation from the power of sin. It is God's plan to keep our hearts undefiled. It's so much easier to keep "the stove" clean than it is to work against the dried-up, crusty filth of sin!

As we accept this relationship, we must develop it so that God's power will rest upon us. This development comes as we learn to love God and live for others. As you develop spiritually, God will lead you. This leading is not only year to year, but moment by moment. As you follow this leading, you will be submitting to what is referred to as the will of God.

For many, God's will seems to be something for which we tend to search, somehow expecting God to give us an A-B-C plan for us to follow. But it isn't something that we happen to find one day; it is something we *live* every day, doing what we know to be right for today while leaving tomorrow in God's hands. Waiting on God's timing and direction can be one of the hardest things to do, but Romans 12:1-2 gives us Three Dedications that *we* can make which will help us discern God's direction today.

Let's look at a dissected and defined explanation of our chapter key verse found in Romans 12:1-2. It reads,

> *I beseech you* [I beg you] *therefore, brethren* [Christians], *by the mercies of God, that ye present your bodies a living sacrifice, holy, acceptable unto God, which is your reasonable service* [the least that we can do]. *And be not conformed to this world: but be ye transformed by the renewing* [rearranging] *of your mind, that ye may prove what is that good, and acceptable, and perfect, will of God.*

Dedication One—Dedicate our Bodies to God: PRESENTATION

I beseech you therefore, brethren, by the mercies of God, that ye present your bodies... Presentation of our bodies [lives] is the foundational dedication upon which the next two dedications will build. It's the first step we can take.

Paul, the writer of Romans, calls the presentation of our bodies a "reasonable service." Why do you suppose that it would be considered a "reasonable service"? Because of the "mercies of God"! It was God's mercy that allowed *His* Son to present *His own* body as a sacrifice for us! The least we can do is give our lives back to Him.

First Peter 1:3 says, *Blessed be the God and Father of our Lord Jesus Christ, which according to his abundant mercy hath begotten us again unto a lively hope by the resurrection of Jesus Christ from the dead.* It is God's abundant mercy that has given us new life and the hope of eternal life in heaven.

Paul is simply saying in Romans, "I am begging you to do what I am about to tell you to do, if for no other reason than the fact that God has shown us so much mercy that it is the least we can do for Him!"

So, what kind of a sacrifice should this be? Paul gives three requirements for a proper sacrifice.

The Presentation of Our Life to God Should Be a Willing Sacrifice.

Again, consider the opening phrases of Romans 12:1: *I beseech you therefore, brethren, by the mercies of God, that ye present your bodies...* We must present ourselves willingly. God did not make us robots. We have the incredible tool of a free will. God in His omnipotence has all rights and ability to control our lives, but how much more precious it is to Him when we willingly present them to Him!

To better understand what a willing sacrifice is, let's look at the story of Abraham and Isaac. Isaac was Abraham's promised son for whom he had waited for many years. God gave Isaac to Abraham when Abraham was 100 years old! Yet several years later, God told Abraham to go to a certain mountaintop, build an altar, and offer a sacrifice-the life of his son. The one thing that Abraham cherished above all, God was asking him to sacrifice! Remember that we are talking about a strong, teenage boy. His father is at least 115 years old now. Nevertheless, Abraham willingly rose up early the next morning with his son and headed toward the mountain to sacrifice Isaac to the Lord. The Bible tells us that Abraham believed God could raise Isaac from the dead (Heb. 11:17-19). However, he was still willing to give that sacrifice with no guarantee of return.

Let's pick up the story here in Genesis 22:9-10:

> *And they came to the place which God had told him of; and Abraham built an altar there, and laid the wood in order, and bound Isaac his son, and laid him*

on the altar upon the wood. And Abraham stretched forth his hand, and took the knife to slay his son.

Think about what's happening here. We have a very old man telling his son that he is about to burn his body as a sacrifice unto God, and we have a strapping, strong teenage boy who could have easily overtaken his father in resistance. However, Isaac willingly allowed his father to bind him and place him on the altar. He was willing to be sacrificed without a struggle.

I have found, in my years of counseling struggling students, that we want God to free us from our addictions, but we are unwilling to sacrifice certain areas of our fleshly desires. We want a clean stove, but we refuse to take action against certain kinds of filth. It's like we're saying, "Oh, I love how clean that part of the stove looks where that nasty chili sauce used to be. But can we please leave the hamburger grease on this part of the stove alone?"

I think we all fall into this trap sometimes. Are there things that you are struggling to do that you know are right, but it just seems there's always a good reason why you can't? Friend, it's not so much a struggle to do what's right; it's more of an unwillingness to make sacrifices for God. Are you unwilling to read your Bible? Are you unwilling to study your Bible? Are you unwilling to memorize your Bible? Are you unwilling to meditate on your Bible? Are you unwilling to hear the Bible taught? You will never do the things God wants you to do until you do the things God wants you to do even when you don't want to.

God will not force us to serve Him. However, God does allow us to go through incredible suffering to bring us to a point in our lives when we will finally say, "Okay, God! I'll stop fighting and I'll climb up on that altar." Many times we are waiting for God to do what God is waiting for us to do. We want God to take away our addictions or temptations, but He wants us to forsake them. He wants us to say no to our flesh. We have fed the flesh and its desires, so now we must willingly sacrifice our flesh by willingly starving it.

It is encouraging to me to know God recognizes that when we give our lives to Him, it is a sacrifice. When we give our entire beings to Him and say, "God, I want you to do with me whatever you please," He knows it's not going to be easy for us. But He faithfully rewards a life sacrificed to Him with a renewed life worth sacrificing for.

The Presentation of Our Life to God Should Be Holy

I beseech you therefore, brethren, by the mercies of God, that ye present your bodies a living sacrifice, holy... How can a life be a holy sacrifice? First Peter 1:15-16 says, B*ut as he which hath called you is holy, so be ye holy in all manner of conversation* [conduct] *Because it is written, Be ye holy; for I am holy.* Our lives should be holy, without evidence of a double standard. We represent Christ to the world. You may be the only Christian someone knows. Your conduct, or way of life, needs to exemplify Christ-likeness!

Romans 6:12-13 reads,

> *Let not sin therefore reign in your mortal body* [don't let sin control your life], *that ye should obey it in the lusts thereof. Neither yield ye your members* [your hands, eyes, tongue, feet] *as instruments of unrighteousness unto sin: but yield yourselves unto God as those that are alive from the dead, and your members as instruments of righteousness unto God.*

In other words, when we die to ourselves, and sacrifice our lives to God, Christ will live through us! Now, each member of your body will be an instrument of righteousness. When our presentation is holy, that simply means that our *lifestyle* should show that we are making a *willing* sacrifice so that Christ may shine from within us.

The Presentation of Our Life to God Should Be Acceptable Unto God

I beseech you therefore, brethren, by the mercies of God, that ye present your bodies a living sacrifice, holy, acceptable unto God...

In Genesis 4, we see the account of Cain and Abel, two sons of Adam and Eve:

> *And in process of time it came to pass, that Cain brought of the fruit of the ground an offering unto the LORD. And Abel, he also brought of the firstlings of his flock and of the fat thereof. And the LORD had respect unto Abel and to his offering: But unto Cain and to his offering he had not respect.* (Gen. 4:3-5)

Both sons brought an offering to God. Abel and his offering were accepted; Cain and his offering were not. Why? Attitude! The Bible tells us in 1 John 3:12 that Cain was a wicked man whose works were evil. By contrast, Abel was a righteous man, as evidenced by the description of his offering: he gave the best of the best of what he had. Cain's proud and arrogant self-righteousness negated any good qualities his offering may have had. Abel's sacrifice was more excellent than Cain's in God's sight, and the difference was faith. (Heb. 11:4)

> *And Cain was very wroth, and his countenance fell. And the LORD said unto Cain, Why art thou wroth? and why is thy countenance fallen? If thou doest well, shalt thou not be accepted? And if thou doest not well, sin lieth at the door. And unto thee shall be his desire, and thou shalt rule over him.* (Gen. 4:5-7)

Although God encouraged him to do well, Cain allowed his selfish motives to lead him into an angry state of depression. The end result of his attitude was the murdering of his own brother! The consequence of presenting an unacceptable sacrifice to God is shown in verse 7: *sin lieth at the door.* Cain's life is a perfect example of that.

So, how can we make sure that our sacrifices are acceptable? It's this simple: an acceptable sacrifice requires that something must die. What is it that must die? Us! We must put to death our pride, our self-ishness, and all of our motives for personal advancement. We must be willing to die to self on a daily basis.

Are you willing to follow Abel's example of faith? Are you willing to give God the best of the best of your life? Are you willing to be proven as acceptable to God?

Our first dedication for discovering God's direction is to dedicate our lives as willing, holy, and acceptable sacrifices. If we will dedicate our lives to Him, God's power will change our stubborn wills, our unholy conduct, and our selfish possession-centeredness.

Dedication Two—Dedicate Your Mind to Knowing God Personally: TRANSFORMATION

…but be ye transformed by the renewing of your mind….

You'll notice that I am skipping a chunk of our key verse (*and be not conformed to this world*), but I believe that the second part of that phrase, *but be ye transformed by the renewing of your mind,* must come before the Conformation (Dedication Three). We cannot "un-conform" ourselves from the world until we are first transformed in our mind. Once God begins to transform our mind, then we can "un-conform" to the world. We will never change the way we act until we change the way we think. Therefore, Dedication Two is Transformation-the dedication of our minds to developing a dynamic relationship with God.

To better understand Dedication Two, allow me to define two of the words in this verse.

- **Transformed:** a change in form; a metamorphosis
- **Renewing:** to revive or reawaken

So Romans 12:2 is saying that a change in our lives will come by the reviving or reawakening of our mind. Therefore, our second dedication is to dedicate [set apart for sacred use] our minds toward God.

Why do you suppose that transformation [a change in form] deals with our mind rather than our actions? The reason is because the way we think defines OR determines what we do. Proverbs 23:7 says, *For as* [a man] *thinketh in his heart, so is he.* God's way of thinking is often 180 degrees in opposition from the way man thinks. Isaiah 55:9 says, *For as the heavens are higher than the earth, so are my ways higher than your ways, and my thoughts than your thoughts.*

When I came back to the Lord after years of living in addiction, I got involved in my local church. I was doing the things I knew I should be doing-reading my Bible, memorizing Scripture, praying, going to church, etc. I soon gained the lofty title of Activities Director of my Single Adults Sunday School class. I was sure this was God's calling on my life. I had big dreams of serving the Lord in the singles ministry. However, something got in the way of this--I met my future wife. Obviously, this eventually put an end to my days of being the Activities Director of the Singles Department.

This is just a simple illustration of the omniscience of God's thinking versus our thinking. I was being obedient in the areas that God had shown me; and though I thought I could clearly see what God had called me to do, God had different plans. His ways were higher than mine. My thoughts were not His thoughts. His next opportunity for me was a Friday night Bible study for addicts that I called Reformers Unanimous. I'm glad my thinking was overruled by God's thinking.

God may have plans for you which are higher than you could ever imagine possible. However, unless you are willing to give your thoughts over to God and trust Him to guide you, His direction for you will be limited. Proverbs 3:5-6 reminds us, *Trust in the LORD with all thine heart; and lean not unto thine own understanding. In all thy ways acknowledge him, and he shall direct thy paths.* His ways and thoughts are higher than yours. Trust that He knows what's best and be willing to submit whatever area in your life He may be asking you to give to Him.

Another reason it is so important to dedicate our thought process to God is because when God sees our sinful thought lives, it grieves Him. Our evil thoughts break His heart. During the days of Noah, Genesis 6:5-6 records that *God saw that the wickedness of man was great in the earth, and that every imagination of the thoughts of his heart was only evil continually. And it repented the LORD that he had made man on the earth.* Man's mind was so wicked that it repented God that He had created man!

You may be thinking right now, "My thought life isn't that bad. I'm okay." But Jeremiah 17:9 says *The heart is deceitful above all things, and desperately wicked: who can know it?* To put it very bluntly, our hearts are so wicked, we can't even know the full extent of that wickedness. If we want to see our hearts' wickedness, we need to ask God to show it to us. Psalm 139:23-24 reads, *Search me, O God, and know my heart: try me, and know my thoughts: And see if there be any wicked way in me, and lead me in the way everlasting.* God's Word is what will reveal our true thoughts and intentions. Hebrews 4:12 says, *For the word of God... is a discerner of the thoughts and intents of the heart.* God's Word! That is what will keep our hearts tender to God and to His leading. It will help us keep our minds pure.

Would you try to clean a greasy, sticky stove with nothing but your bare hands? Probably not. You'd be sure you had a good scrub cloth and cleanser to tackle that stove. To do anything else would be a monumental waste of time and effort. It's the same in keeping our hearts and minds pure. You can't do it on your own. Everyone needs the cleansing power of God's Word.

Our lives are wrecked by sin. We bear the scars from our past. But Isaiah 55:7 says, *Let the wicked forsake his way, and the unrighteous man his thoughts: and let him return unto the LORD, and he will have mercy upon him; and to our God, for he will abundantly pardon.* The cure given here for the unrighteous man forsaking his thoughts is returning to the Lord!

Proverbs 16:3 teaches an incredible principle regarding the sacrificing of our lives. This verse reads, *Commit thy works unto the LORD, and thy <u>thoughts shall be established</u>*. By committing our efforts [works] to the Lord, our thoughts will change. The previous verse in Proverbs 16 says, *All the ways of a man are clean in his own eyes; but the LORD weigheth the spirits*. We may think we are doing okay, or something may look "clean" in our eyes, but God looks from within at the inner man. He sees the heart. Therefore, we need to commit our works to God (i.e., be willing to do what God tells us to do, even if we don't understand why). Then, after we do our part, God will establish our thoughts. **We will never change the way we act until we let God change the way we think.**

My first New Year's Eve after giving my life to God, I had an unforgettable experience. Though I was striving for victory over addictions, I still fell regularly. An announcement had been made in our church about an all-night activity to celebrate New Year's Eve. I made plans to attend. I was looking forward to a good, clean and sober New Year's Eve. However, when I arrived, I received a big shock: it was a teen activity! With utter embarrassment I began retreating from the gymnasium with every intention to go to a party at an old friend's house.

Just then, the church's youth pastor grabbed me and asked me to help with crowd control. "We've got more kids than we thought we were going to have," he said. I was thinking, *Crowd control... junior highers... New Year's Eve... they just don't go together.* But I agreed. We played volleyball, basketball, indoor mini-putt, and at 2:00 a.m., we watched *Dennis the Menace*. Only one person stayed up all night: me. I guess it was because I had a little more practice than those kids had at staying up all night! But what was unforgettable and unbelievable to me was I had the time of my life that evening with those kids!

As I drove home from the activity that morning, my heart was overflowing with joy. I had had both a sober night and a great time! As I pulled up to a stoplight, I saw some of my drug buddies on their way home from the party I almost went to. Unbeknownst to them, I was watching them; to my sorrow, I saw the shame, agony, and misery on their faces. I broke down and cried.

That day I saw the metamorphosis that was happening in my mind as I was committing my works to the Lord. My way of thinking was changing as I was doing what I knew to be right, as understood by reading God's Word and hearing it preached. This change in my mind was beginning to take the knowledge I had about God and was transforming it into a dynamic relationship with God. As a result of this relationship, I was able to recognize God's leading through dedication number three.

Dedication Three—Dedicate Ourselves to God's Standard: CONFORMATION

And be not conformed to this world...

The very first Dedication is presenting ourselves to God as a sacrifice that is willing, holy, and acceptable-Presentation. Then, we dedicate our minds to God's Word by changing the way we think-Transformation. Our third Dedication is the devotion of ourselves to God's standard-Conformation. Our text verse says, *And be not conformed to this world.* What does "not being conformed to the world" mean? Unconformity to the world means that we should not be poured into the world's mold.

Why is this so dangerous? Think about it: The world's ways and philosophies are always changing. It wasn't that long ago when teen-age pregnancy was nearly unheard of, much less, teenage abortions! Now, both are commonplace because society's standards of morality have changed. However, God's standard of morality never changes. As believers, we cannot afford to continue forming ourselves into the world's way of conducting our lives. Just because the world thinks it's okay to act one way doesn't mean God feels the same way.

We are to be conformed to something completely different from the world's design, and that means being conformed to God's design. Remember 2 Timothy 3:16: *All scripture is given by inspiration of*

God, and is profitable [its main use is] *for doctrine* [what is right], *for reproof* [what's not right], *for correction* [how to get right], *for instruction in righteousness* [how to stay right]. So the Bible's main purpose is to tell those of us who are believers what is right, what is not right, how to get right, and how to stay right. We use the Bible to determine what conduct is right and what conduct is wrong.

The next verse goes on to say, *That the man of God* [Christian] *may be perfect* [maturing], *thoroughly furnished unto all good works.* That's exactly what conformation is-maturing our lives into God's design using God's Word as a road map and the Holy Spirit as our driver!

First John 2:15 further warns us against being conformed to the world's standards. *Love not the world, neither the things that are in the world. If any man love the world, the love of the Father is not in him.* We cannot be conformed to the world and please God at the same time. It is impossible.

Do standards matter? Let's think about our illustration of a clean stove. When you're cooking on a stove, whose standards for "clean" do you want to use? The standards that say filth doesn't matter, or the standards that make you take some elbow grease and quality cleaning tools to the appliance you use to prepare food for your family and you? Make no mistake; standards matter!

Romans 8:28-29 are two verses that almost everybody has memorized and, at times, have claimed. However, we rarely take note of its significance toward defining God's purpose for our lives. These verses tell us, *And we know that all things work together for good to them that love God, to them who are the called according to his purpose. For whom he did foreknow, he also did predestinate to be conformed to the image of his Son.*

Now, what does "all" mean? *All* means all, and that's all that it means. So, we know that all things in our lives work together for good if we are called to His purpose. In verse 29 is the explanation of the purpose for which God has called us: to be conformed to the image of His Son!

However, the flip side of this truth is that if we are not conforming to the image of God's Son, then we are not being called according to His purpose. Therefore we cannot claim the promise that all things will work together for good in our lives! When we turn our lives over to God [presentation], God is able to work all things in our past, present, and future together for His good. Let me warn you, however, that if you are not willing to conform your life to Christ, don't expect everything to work together for good. Chances are, they will not.

Part of conforming to God's image means letting go of our past grievances. We often want to hang on to past hurts that God wants us to release and allow Him to work them out for His good! Ephesians 4:31 says, *Let all bitterness* [compressed feelings], *and wrath* [feelings of getting even], *and anger, and clamour* [arguing], *and evil speaking* [gossiping], *be put away from you, with all malice* [a desire for physical injury]. If we allow these emotions to build up, they will slowly destroy us. The phrase *be put away from you* has behind it the idea of incarceration. Send them away and lock them up from ever returning again.

Verse 32 of Ephesians 4 holds the key to letting go of past grievances: *And be ye kind one to another* [outward expression of feelings], *tenderhearted* [inward expression], *forgiving one another* [upward expression], *even as God for Christ's sake hath forgiven you.* The phrase *even as God for Christ's sake hath forgiven you* is somewhat similar to the "reasonable service" we spoke of earlier. Surely if God can love us enough to give His own Son to pay our penalty for sin… if God can love us enough to give us freedom from the power of sin … if God can love us enough to give us an eternal home in heaven… we can most certainly let go of past hurts and grievances and be *kind one to another* (on the outside), *tenderhearted* (on the inside), *and forgiving one another*!

Let go of past feelings that you may use to justify your wrongdoing. Incarcerate them! I know this is a touchy subject because we're talking about our emotional makeup. But if you will learn to harness your emotions for the glory of our Lord Jesus Christ and for His good, I promise you that freedom is inevitable! A life filled with joy is the end result, rather than these destructive feelings that we bottle up inside of ourselves. We must let God have control of our emotions. Let go, and let God be in control.

Properly controlled emotions show others that our strength is in Christ. Proverbs 16:32 says, *He that is slow to anger is better than the mighty; and he that ruleth his spirit* [temperament] *than he that taketh a city.* One who is slow to anger and controls his spirit is one who controls his emotions. But that control doesn't come from within one's self; it comes from God. Such a person practices Ephesians 4:31-32. According to Proverbs 16:32, this person is better than the mighty! He has more control than an army of soldiers!

Conversely, if we lose control of our emotions, we are vulnerable to Satan's attacks. Proverbs 25:28 says, *He that hath no rule over his own spirit* [temperament], *is like a city that is broken down, and without walls.* Old Testament cities had walls built around them to protect them from the enemy. Without the walls, these cities would have no protection from their enemies. When we don't control our emotions and we allow those Ephesians 4:31 feelings to creep into our lives, we are open to the attacks of the enemy, and so are those who depend on us for their own protection.

Of course, controlling our emotions will build a wall that will protect us from the influences and attacks of the enemy. Remember, though, once those walls come back down, we are immediately unprotected and vulnerable emotionally.

If we want to overcome attacks, and if we want to keep ourselves from being vulnerable, we must not lose control of our emotions. It's not the loss of control that conquers us; it is the loss of protection from the attacks of Satan that will conquer us. The world's mold is led by emotions. God's mold will control our emotions. Thus, to conform to the image of God we will be under the control of God's emotions, not our own.

How the Three Dedications Help in Discerning God's Direction

Three Dedications -- Presentation, Transformation, and Conformation. Now, how do these help us discern God's direction? Let's look at our key verse for this principle again.

Romans 12:1-2 says,

> *I beseech you therefore, brethren, by the mercies of God, that ye* (Dedication One) *present your bodies a living sacrifice, holy, acceptable unto God, which is your reasonable service.* (Dedication Three) *And be not conformed to this world: but* (Dedication Two) *be ye transformed by the renewing of your mind, that ye may prove what is that good, and acceptable, and perfect, will of God.*

In other words, we will know God's perfect direction for our lives if these three areas are dedicated to God. Maintain these Three Dedications and God's direction will always remain clear. Though we may not see the future, we will know God's desire for the present.

A frequent question is, "How can I know God's will for my life?" It's really simple. God's will is a day-by-day process; these dedications are a day-by-day process. We do our part by committing to these Three Dedications, and God will do the rest by working His will out in our lives. Anytime you may struggle with foolishly thinking that God has forgotten about you, or He doesn't really care for you anymore, or you feel separated from or out of touch with God, investigate these three areas in your life. It may be that there is a Dedication missing on your part.

First Peter 4:1-2 reads,

> *Forasmuch then as Christ hath suffered for us in the flesh, arm yourselves likewise with the same mind: for he that hath suffered in the flesh hath ceased from*

sin; That he no longer should live the rest of his time in
the flesh to the lusts of men, but to the will of God.

Because Jesus Christ suffered in the flesh for us (having no sin in His life), we should take upon ourselves the same mind of Christ! When we live in the mind of Christ, we will not live in the lusts of men, but in the center of God's will. That's the best place to be!

Devote yourself to these Three Dedications today! Present yourself to God as a living sacrifice. Commit yourself to the transforming of your mind to the mind of Christ. Determine that you will not be conformed to the mold of the world; rather, accept conformity to God's standard of living. After all, it's so much easier to keep your heart clean than it is to clean the heart after it has been defiled.

We Cannot Fight a Fleshly Appetite by Indulging in It.

Be not deceived: God is not mocked: for whatsoever a man soweth, that shall he also reap. For he that soweth to his flesh shall of the flesh reap corruption: but he that soweth to the Spirit shall of the Spirit reap life everlasting.
—Galatians 6:7-8

An appetite is a dangerous thing. If disciplined, it can be controlled. If not, it can control an individual. God has given within each of His children a power to control our appetites. The need for food, drink, and sexual satisfaction are all God-given, legitimate needs. Satan, however, will twist them into lusts which, when coupled with enticement, lead to a life of sin and spiritual and sometimes physical death. This pattern is spelled out in James 1:14-16: *But every man is tempted, when he is drawn away of his own lust, and enticed. Then when lust hath conceived, it bringeth forth sin: and sin, when it is finished, bringeth forth death. Do not err, my beloved brethren.*

Stated simply, we cannot fight a fleshly appetite by indulging in it. Disregarding this principle has caused such great pain and failure for many years. It is also this very same principle that God will bring to our remembrance every time we feel like indulging in any fleshly desire. This principle has done more to discourage the desire to wander than any of the others. If the truth be known, the failure to recognize and apply this principle to our lives is usually at the core of every besetting sin.

Remember the old commercial that advertised KOOL cigarettes? The ad (falsely) stated that "They Satisfy." Well, if this were true, then we could all smoke one KOOL cigarette, our appetite would be satisfied, and we would never need to indulge that appetite again. The truth is that KOOL cigarettes (as do all cigarettes) never satisfy. The appetite created with indulgence will only intensify. Indulging in any fleshly appetite only makes it stronger, never weaker.

Not too long ago, I listened to a documentary on starving children in the Third World. My heart broke as the narrator explained that though the children were starving, they do not feel the hunger pains that we feel right before dinnertime. Rather, they have suppressed their appetite for so long that their starvation is not accompanied with the pain of hunger.

It is the same way with any fleshly desire that we struggle with. Whether it be cigarettes, drugs, alcohol, overeating, adulterous thoughts, pornography, gambling, or any other crippling appetite, if we do not feed it, do not give in to it, it will die. The only way to destroy the appetite is to starve it. That is a promise from God.

So the next time you feel that urge to indulge in a sinful fleshly desire, resign yourself to just "skip that meal." When you skip a meal, you will see that after a few minutes or hours, you have lost your appetite for that meal. You may not be able to skip every meal, but eventually your desire will starve itself to death and the hunger will be gone. Don't let the devil tell you if you just have one more cigarette or just one more drink or one more chocolate bar, you will be satisfied.

Reformers Unanimous' Principle #4 of 10 reminds us that it is not possible to fight a fleshly appetite by indulging in it. We cannot feed selfish, fleshly appetites and find any level of satisfaction whatsoever. Ecclesiastes 5:10 teaches us that *He that loveth silver shall not be satisfied with silver; nor he that loveth abundance with increase: this is also vanity.* If you are looking for satisfaction from the accumulation of money or the accumulation of possessions, your search will be in vain; it will equal nothing. Solomon goes on to teach in verse eleven that *When goods increase, they are increased that eat them: and what good is there to the owners thereof, saving the beholding of them with their eyes?* The disappointment of having relatives, friends, enemies, and Uncle Sam seeking to take advantage of your fortune will outweigh the useful benefits of everything you have sought to gain.

At eighteen years of age, a young man had one ambition in life—to become rich and famous, gaining all that the world has to offer. That young man set out in a rock 'n roll career that within a few years had given him all that he could want. His fans numbered in the hundreds of thousands; there was no earthly pleasure that was withheld from him. While heading toward the peak of his fame and glory, when anything he desired was at his fingertips, he wrote the now-infamous self-portrait song, "(I Can't Get No) Satisfaction." Though Mick Jagger had successfully gained all the fame and fortune that the world claims will bring satisfaction, he discovered that ultimately it will not bring a man lasting pleasure. To this day, I would probably safely assume that he has failed to find true satisfaction in life, though he has famously fed his every appetite.

The Law of Sowing and Reaping: Actions Have Consequences

It seems natural for us to believe that a focus on meeting our own selfish desires will improve <u>our chances of providing ourselves pleasure</u>. But why is it so true that earthly possessions fail to provide lasting pleasure? Because of this very important principle: Bad things in life are enjoyed first and paid for later, but good things in life are paid for first and enjoyed later. I think most of us have seen this principle to be true in our own lives. Hebrews 11:25 tells us that sin is pleasurable, but only for a season. We have all made wrong choices that seemed to bring great pleasure at the time. But when the harvest came and we began reaping the consequences of our choices, we begged God for a crop failure! We enjoyed the wrong pleasures first and had to unwillingly pay for them later.

However, the opposite is true as well. The right pleasures are paid for first then enjoyed for the rest of our lives. It requires sowing the seeds of effort and righteousness. We will then reap a harvest of pleasure that can be enjoyed forever. The right pleasures do not consist of what pleases us but rather of whom we should be seeking to please. Pleasing God will bring us pleasure beyond compare – definitely far above the pleasures of this world.

Our problem is not so much our continuing struggle with sin that slows our progress in the Christian walk. The real problem is that we fail to serve our new governing Authority. What would happen if we would simply "indulge" in obedience to God rather than indulge in those things that have made us a nation of addicts?

We tend to believe that we can do good without following our new Ruler. When we do this, we not only frustrate God's grace [God's great plan for us], but we also frustrate ourselves. We fail to achieve the progress in our Christian lives that we had hoped to achieve by our righteous living, and we become discouraged with ourselves. We forget that, being dead, we are helpless without this new and pure, living Authority ruling our lives. Without this Authority, we will almost certainly indulge the very appetites of the flesh we want to escape. In Romans 7:24, Paul cries out in frustration, *O wretched man that I am! who shall deliver me from the body of this death?*

Without God, we are nothing. Yet, we often foolishly attempt to accomplish our good works or make great feats of righteous living in our own strength. We indulge our own egos before we submit to God's authority. Before God can do anything with us, we must first come to the conclusion that without God's power on us, we are helpless. Without submission to His rule over our lives, we are helpless in overcoming the strongholds that sin (our former ruler) attempts to bring back into our lives. The power to gain such victories comes only through Christ living in us. His rule over us gives us the strength we need to resist the lure and allure of our former ruler. A verse so often quoted, Philippians 4:13, says *I can do all things through Christ which strengtheneth me.* Oh, how often we forget how helpless we are without the strength of Christ!

When I was running from the Lord and my addictions were crippling my life, I would cry out to God, "Why did You let this happen to me? Why won't You protect me from the devil? Can't You take away this temptation?" But I – not God – had put myself in that position. Galatians 6:7-8 says, *Be not deceived* [misled]; *God is not mocked* [imitated]: *for whatsoever a man soweth* [scatters], *that shall he also reap. For he that soweth to his flesh shall of the flesh reap corruption; but he that soweth to the Spirit shall of the Spirit reap life everlasting.*

Let's dissect this verse and define the words so that we can have a greater understanding of what God is trying to teach us.

***Be not deceived* [misled]; *God is not mocked* [imitated]...** How do we imitate God? We imitate God when we live as if we control our own consequences for our wrongdoings. I made this mistake many times in my early flight to find freedom. I would go out for the evening, planning to enjoy myself. Yet I knew that if I allowed myself to walk out the door, I was going to do something before the night was over that was against the law and a sin against God. I knew that I would struggle with drugs and alcohol. However, I foolishly believed that if I controlled the atmosphere in which I indulged in these sinful things, somehow I could control the consequences of it. If I could keep myself from drinking too much, then I would not get a DUI. I could participate in drugs, but hide it well enough so the cops would not find out.

I was convinced that I could control the consequences of my choices. I mocked God. I imitated God by acting as if I had the power to control each and every circumstance. But, who truly is in control of everything? God is, of course. I lived as if I had no ruling authority within me. I forgot I was helpless.

...for whatsoever a man soweth [scatters], *that shall he also reap* [receive in return]. Farming, of course, is a great example of the Law of Sowing and Reaping. When a farmer goes to his field to plant his crop, he sows his seed. Figuratively speaking, that is what we do as we live out our lives. We leave distinctive paths behind us. Those paths are what we have sown. The seed will then ripen until harvest. It always does; it never fails. We will reap the fruit of whatever seed we sow. If a farmer plants corn, he will not reap green beans. So, the produce of whatever a man leaves scattered behind him is exactly what that man will eventually receive. Galatians 6:8 goes on to say, *For he that soweth to his flesh* [desires] *shall of the flesh reap corruption; but he that soweth to the Spirit shall of the Spirit reap life everlasting.* The man that lives for his own desires will reap ruin, but the man that lives under the control of the Holy Spirit (his new Ruler) will reap an abundant life.

We are responsible for where we are today. We are reaping what we have previously sown. Do not be misled. God is not going to be imitated. We can live neither righteously nor unrighteously without yielding our "followship." We will either choose to follow our former ruler and reap ruin, or we will choose to follow the new Ruler within us and reap life. For whatever we leave behind in our lives, we will receive back the results of those same deeds. If we sow fleshly choices and actions, we will reap fleshly results. We are helpless. We cannot live righteously without yielding to our new Ruler, and we will not live sinfully without first submitting to our former ruler.

Our willingness to submit to the leading of our former ruler is what put us in this position of helplessness – not God; He is our helper. "Helper" is the definition of the Comforter (see John 14:16-18). He will help us reap life if we will sow submission to Him.

Let's take a look at the descending path of sowing to the flesh. First, we were deceived. You may ask, "How could I allow the devil to deceive me?" It's very simple. You see, Satan sows and reaps, too. When the devil plants a deceitful thought in your mind, you have the option to either accept it or reject it. *Be not deceived...* The choice is yours alone whether to be deceived or not.

Proverbs 3:5 says, *Trust in the LORD with all thine heart; and lean not unto thine own understanding.* When you give consideration to a deceitful thought and begin reasoning within yourself to justify it, you are handing the devil a building permit to start immediate construction of a stronghold in your mind. This will always lead to corruption in your heart. It will make you far more susceptible to compromise in your actions. Remember, the heart is the seat of belief. The Bible indicates that a stronghold in the mind exists when we choose to believe something to be true which contradicts the Word of God (see 2 Cor. 10:3-5). Hebrews 3:12 says *Take heed, brethren, lest there be in any of you an evil heart of unbelief, in departing from the living God.* It is very easy to be deceived when we stop believing the Truth. That is why we are so helpless without God.

After we were deceived, we then sowed our seed. Second Corinthians 9:6 says ...*He which soweth sparingly shall reap also sparingly; and he which soweth bountifully shall reap also bountifully.* If we have bountifully scattered seeds of destruction behind us, we will reap that same destruction at some point in our lives. We cannot fight a fleshly appetite by indulging in it.

I have made many bad decisions. These decisions were always the result of errors in my thinking. I was thinking with my deceived mind and it led me to yielding to the wrong authority. The key to sowing the right seed is yielding to the inner man rather than the outer man. By God's grace, I finally realized I needed to change my decision-making process. Seeing my need for guidance and direction, I began looking to God's Word to lead me in my decisions. Heeding the Bible helps us to avoid satanic deception.

To protect yourself from being deceived, which leads to sowing the wrong seed, check your emotions, your thoughts, and your desires with the Bible. That's where your answers will be found. Remember 2 Timothy 3:16? *All scripture is given by inspiration of God, and is profitable for doctrine, for reproof, for correction, for instruction in righteousness.* The Bible's intention is to show us what is right [doctrine], what is not right [reproof], how to get right [correction], and how to stay right [instruction in righteousness].

Before God can do anything with our lives, we must reaffirm that without the help of God and His Word, we are helpless. But there is hope! Protect yourself from deception by following God's guidance.

Realize Your New Identity in Christ: Sow Choices That Show Christ

...nevertheless I live; yet not I, but Christ liveth in me.

When we were crucified with Christ, our subordinate members were no longer under obligation to submit to the ruling authority of sin. Rather, we are re-created in the image of Christ. Our members are now instructed by the Word of Truth and the Spirit of Truth to submit to our new ruling Authority. This is how God wants us to live. The Spirit of God that has quickened [made alive] your spirit will now guide you and direct you into all truth (Ps. 32:8). The choices you sow under the influence of the Holy Spirit will show Christ. They will reflect your new identity in Him. They will deny the appetites of the flesh.

Submission to this inner Leader is referred to in our passage as Christ living in us. That is the manifestation of our new creation in Christ. We are no longer forced into submission to the body of sin. Instead, we are given the opportunity to yield in submission to the indwelling Holy Spirit. We do not have to work our way to righteousness in our own power. God is leading us into the paths of righteousness, and He is doing it for His name's sake (Ps. 23:3)!

In 2 Corinthians 5:17 Paul records this truth concerning the regime change within us: *Therefore if any man be in Christ, he is a new creature: old things are passed away; behold, all things are become new.* I have heard people argue that this verse is not referring to the "old man" passing away and a "new man" coming alive, but rather it is referring to the old covenant [the law] passing away and the new covenant [grace] replacing it. I would tend to agree that, in context, this is referring to the end of the law and the replacement of God's new covenant of grace. However, the truth of this passage is just as real as if the former view were being discussed here. Therefore, Paul is actually telling us that since we are in Christ, we are literally new creatures. The old covenant of man doing the work is passed away and has been replaced with the new covenant where God does the work. Amen!

I am so sick of this "try hard to do better" mentality that is permeating our churches and Christian schools. It is why Fundamentalist Christianity is so attacked by the seldom churched with charges of legalism. When it comes to justification, we all agree that Christ did the work, but when it comes to sanctification, we somehow believe that we must row our own canoe. We think the ability to live righteously is found in our effort and will power. That is not true; it is nothing more than legalistic sanctification. Christ's substitutionary death paid our penalty for sin and emancipated us from the power of sin. Christ's death paid our penalty; Christ's resurrection freed us from sin's power. A paid penalty is justification; emancipation is sanctification.

When we fail to understand our new identity in Christ, we lose focus on how to walk in victory. It becomes far easier to slip back into the patterns and choices that indulge the flesh rather than feed the inner man. We are not so much required to do well as we are requested to yield to His leading. John 15:7 reads, *If ye abide in me...ye shall ask what ye will, and it shall be done unto you.* That's like saying, "If you cooperate with Me, things will happen for your benefit." He is willing to lead a cooperative subordinate. He will not force you to follow Him. If you know His voice is calling, you should follow.

It is a wonderful privilege to be a Christian! When we understand God's management systems, we will better understand who we are and how He intends to use us. Earlier, we discussed this understanding process as the need to transform our minds. *Transform* means "to metamorphose; to change the character, nature, condition, etc., of something or someone." A transformed life is the product of God-directed transformed choices that no longer feed fleshly appetites.

In the early 1980s I enjoyed watching a television show called *The Incredible Hulk*. It was the comic book story of David Bruce Banner: "Physician... Scientist... searching for a way to tap into the hidden strength that all humans have, when an accidental overdose of gamma-radiation altered his body chemistry. And now, when David Banner becomes angry or outraged, a startling metamorphosis occurs..." They would then close the show's introduction with a view of David Banner becoming angry after injuring himself while changing a flat tire during a storm. Then, turning into a green, muscle-bound monster, he would beat up his car.

Though a silly story, there is a profound truth in this illustration. You see, when God transforms our minds, we begin to understand who we really are in Christ; identity in Christ is personally experienced. This position (in which we do not rule, but rather submit to Him) allows us to experience a startling metamorphosis during times of adversity when, in the past, we may have become frustrated or angry. Realizing our new identity, we may submit to a power greater than ours, one through which we will respond correctly to difficult circumstances. This metamorphosis is Christ in us, *the hope of glory* (Col. 1:27). *Glory* means "to bring the right opinion of." It literally means "to make to look good." Christ living in us is our only hope of ever looking good. God's purpose for us looking good is that we might make Him look good in the process. In other words, we glorify God [make Him look good] when others see this startling metamorphosis occur.

But it only happens when we indulge in faith in Jesus Christ instead of the flesh. That's why we must recognize the power of faith.

Recognize the Power of Faith: Trust God to Help You Reap Change from Sowing Godly Choices

...the life which I now live in the flesh I live by the faith of the Son of God.

Now, of course, understanding that Christ is in us and willing to lead us is not too difficult to accept. However, merely accepting this truth does not produce change. *Belief* is what produces change. Belief in God's substitutionary death of Christ on the cross is what grants us justification, and belief in God's substitutionary placement of Christ in us is what provides us with sanctification. Faith saves and faith produces change. We are so certain of the requirement of faith to produce a convert, but we often overlook the need for faith in Christ's leading in order to produce a changed life.

In our key verse, I am reminded that the life that I now live must be lived by faith–not faith in myself or in my church or in my works, but faith in the very same Son of God who saved my soul from hell. Praise God! His gift keeps giving!

What exactly is faith? I have heard it said that faith is a bold obedience to God's revealed will despite all circumstances. That may be the definition for a level of faith that changes you. But it is not the definition of the faith that saves you. Obedience doesn't produce regeneration. Yet faith does produce regeneration. Thus, faith has two definitions, or measurements. There is the faith that saves you and the faith that changes you. I define faith as, "the personal measurement of my level of confidence in what Christ can and will do in, through, and for us." When we exercise our faith, we are saying, "We are doing this because we believe the result will be exactly what God says it will be." This exercise produces a greater measure of faith.

As we saw in the discussion of Principle #3, God's will is revealed through our Presentation, Conformation, and Transformation (Rom. 12:1-2). When His will is revealed, then real faith is measured by our willingness to step out in *bold* obedience and do as God directs, regardless of the circumstances.

It is important to understand this vital truth: God's acceptance of us cannot be acquired by what we have done for Him, nor can it be lost by what we have failed to do. We receive God's acceptance by having faith in His sacrifice for justification and faith in His guidance for sanctification. There are three aspects of faith that we need to understand to properly exercise our faith. First, **faith depends on its object.** Many people have faith in faith alone, rather than faith in an object. Your faith should be 100 percent dependent on the object in which you are placing that faith. If you have faith that a chair will hold your weight, then you have placed your faith in the object– the chair. You believe it will hold you so you exercise that belief by sitting in it. Many self-help programs in society will tell you to pick something or someone in which to place your faith. If you place your faith in something besides God's system of management, then you will have made the same mistake as those in society who are *Having a form of godliness, but denying the power thereof: from such turn away* (2 Tim. 3:5). Place your faith in Christ alone, both to save you and to lead you. Faith in Him is the *substance of things hoped for, the evidence of things not seen* (Heb, 11:1).

Second, **the depth of our faith is determined by the depth of our knowledge of the object in which we place our faith.** Do you need more faith? Choose to feed your knowledge of your object of faith – God – instead of feeding appetites that can destroy you. How do you "feed" faith? Romans 10:17 says, *So then faith cometh by hearing, and hearing by the word of God.* Your faith and knowledge of God will grow as you are under the teaching and preaching of the Word of God.

I have two friends. Their names are John and Michael. John has been a friend for years. I just met Michael a few months ago. I have a lot of knowledge of John. However, I only know a little bit about Michael. If I needed to lend a one dollar bill to either of them, it would not take much effort on my part to exercise this measure of faith. I have little knowledge of Michael, but I am still willing to lend him something of so little value. However, if I had $100,000 in my pocket and I needed to find someone to entrust it with, I'm going to give it to John because I have more knowledge of him and can exercise my faith *in* him based on my knowledge *of* him.

Similarly, **we only trust God based on how much knowledge we have of Him.** If God asks us for a little, then we oblige Him. If God asks for much, then we hold back. Romans 12:1-2 begs us to give our lives to Him as a living sacrifice. We look at this life as being worth $100,000 and are unwilling to yield. God looks at this life as being worthless and the next life as being of great value. Luke 9:24 reminds us that, *whosoever will save his life shall lose it: but whosoever will lose his life for my sake, the same shall save it.* Because we do not know God well, we are unwilling to make a sacrifice above our current measure of confidence in Him.

Our sacrifice is limited not by what He can do with us, but by what we fail to believe. We do not recognize the power of faith. Hebrews 11:6 says *But without faith it is impossible to please him: for he that cometh to God must believe that he is, and that he is a rewarder of them that diligently seek him.* Our ability to please God is directly related to our faith in Him. When we come to God, we must come *in faith* believing in who God is and believing that He will reward our diligence in seeking Him.

When we desire our will over God's will, we are not exercising faith in God. We have all been guilty of searching for God's direction and, having been shown His direction, we doubted our ability to follow it. Maybe God points out areas of our lives that need to change, or He may call us to the mission field or to change careers. God's pleasure in us comes to a halt the moment we choose to follow our own will with disregard to His direction. At that moment, we cease from exercising faith. We often want God's favor on our lives as a prerequisite to increasing our faith in Him. But it doesn't work that way. The step of faith comes first, then the reward.

Third, **faith is an action word.** Faith says, "I am going to do right." James 2:17-18 says, *Even so faith, if it hath not works, is dead, being alone. Yea, a man may say, Thou hast faith, and I have works: show me thy faith without thy works, and I will show thee my faith by my works.* Our outward actions reveal the inner condition of our faith. *Works* is an old English word for the Modern English word *effort.* Our efforts do not save us, neither do they change us, but they are a by-product of our faith. Faith without works [effort] is dead. We need to recognize faith's power and then exercise that measure of faith. Then, we are feeding our faith with the result being a greater measure of faith.

Matthew 14:25-31 gives us the account of Peter walking on the water. The disciples were out to sea in the middle of the night when a strong storm came. In the midst of the storm, here comes Jesus walking on the water toward them. They thought it was a spirit! But in verse 27, *Jesus spake unto them, saying, Be of good cheer; it is I; be not afraid.* Peter's response was, *Lord, if it be thou, bid me come unto thee on the water. And* [Jesus] *said, Come. And when Peter was come down out of the ship, he walked on the water, to go to Jesus* (Matthew 14:28-29).

Peter's faith was put in action by his immediate obedience to God's call, despite the potential consequences. The Bible goes on to say in verses 30 and 31,

> *But when he saw the wind boisterous, he was afraid; and beginning to sink, he cried, saying, Lord, save me. And immediately Jesus stretched forth his hand, and caught him, and said unto him, O thou of little faith, wherefore didst thou doubt?*

When Peter's eyes were focused on Jesus, he was able to walk in faith. But as soon as he took his eyes off of Jesus and put them on the circumstances around him, he began to sink.

When we take our eyes off of Jesus, our faith is going to waver. Friend, our faith is based on nothing less than Jesus' blood [for justification] and righteousness [for sanctification]. You have died to the power of sin. You are now helpless to live righteously without your new identity, Christ in you. You will feed, rather than fight, fleshly appetites without your new identity in Christ. Recognize that these truths will change your life if you will only believe them. Once believed, simply exercise your faith by relinquishing self-ownership to God.

Relinquish Self-Ownership to God

...the Son of God, who loved me, and gave himself for me.

God gave Himself for me. Not for me to be me, but for me to be like Him. If I give $10,000 for a car, I do not give it so the car can have some spending money. I give it so the car will belong to me and take me wherever I want to go. The same is true with Christ's gift. He gave it to take ownership of us.

To effectively fight fleshly appetites, we must finally relinquish self-ownership to God. We have given Him our hearts by being reborn, and now we must also submit our lives to Him. Without

God's power, we cannot gain freedom in Christ. We have tried to work out our problems, but we just can't do it. The key is to overcome our sinful habits by the power that is within us–the power of the Holy Spirit. Remember, Philippians 4:13 says, *I can do all things through Christ which strengtheneth me.* We must yield our "rights" to Christ and let Him work through us to overcome our sinful habits.

Then, and only then, can we fight and conquer our fleshly appetites.

Small Compromises Lead to Great Disasters, Little Sins Lead to Big Sins.

*He that is faithful
in that which is least is faithful
also in much: and he that is
unjust in the least is unjust
also in much.*

—*Luke 16:10*

So many students and friends of the ministry have asked me questions like this: "Brother Steve, I have stayed away from my old friends, I have stopped acting the way I used to, I even go to church at least once a week, but I still ended up engaging in my addiction. Why doesn't this work?" Such a difficult question to the student, but such an easy answer from God.

I will usually ask them where they are in their Bible reading, Scripture memory, prayer life, mid-week service attendance, witnessing, and what they are doing for service to the kingdom (driving a bus route, cleaning the church, nursery work, and helping others, for example). Without fail, they have fallen away in almost everything. Oddly enough they have fallen away for only two to three weeks, then *bang!* The devil acquires a foothold.

How does this happen? Well, God's answer is found in Luke 16:10: *He that is faithful* [consistent] *in that which is least is faithful* [consistent] *also in much: and he that is unjust in the least is unjust also in much.* According to this verse, if we are consistent or, faithful in all the little things, we will be consistent or faithful in the big things and remain victorious. However, if we are inconsistent in the little things, we will fail in the big things. The reason is simple: God loves the little things. You see, this list of small things determine our master. We cannot serve God and earthly lusts (Matthew 6:24). We will have no choice but to love one and hate the other. The more we do for God, the more we will learn to love Him. And why do we love Him? Because He first loved us!

Remember this: small compromises lead to great disasters. You may compromise your Bible reading, your church attendance, or your kingdom service requirements now, but the consequences are guaranteed to be great. If you are not yielding yourself to the little requests of God, you will yield yourself to the little requests of your enemy—and him alone will you serve. Romans 6:16 tells us, *Know ye not, that to whom ye yield yourselves servants to obey, his servants ye are to whom ye obey; whether of sin unto death, or of obedience unto righteousness?*

Commit today to do the little things every day. You will never read your Bible every day until you read your Bible on the days you don't want to. Commit to the acts of obedience that seem small today. They may become the very actions that keep you from falling into temptation tomorrow, as we will see.

Keep Your Focus

Matthew 14:25-31 gives us the account of Peter walking on the water. The disciples were out to sea in the middle of the night when a strong storm came. In the midst of the storm, here comes Jesus walking on the water toward them. They thought it was a spirit! But in verse 27, *Jesus spake unto them, saying, Be of good cheer; it is I; be not afraid.* Peter's response was, *Lord, if it be thou, bid me come unto thee on the water. And [Jesus] said, Come. And when Peter was come down out of the ship, he walked on the water, to go to Jesus* (Matthew 14:28-29).

Peter's faith was put into action by his immediate obedience to God's call despite the potential consequences. The Bible goes on to say in verses 30 and 31:

> But when he saw the wind boisterous, he was afraid; and beginning to sink, he cried, saying, Lord, save me. And immediately Jesus stretched forth his hand, and caught him, and said unto him, O thou of little faith, wherefore didst thou doubt?

When Peter's eyes were focused on Jesus, he was able to walk in faith. But as soon as he took his eyes off of Jesus and put them on the circumstances around him, he began to sink. When we take our eyes off of Jesus, our faith is going to waver.

This is a question of focus—and unlike Peter, it rarely takes a storm for us to take our eyes off Jesus. Instead, we look away from Him at the slightest distraction. An informercial on television can keep us from prayer. As a result we miss the strength God wants to give us as we pray, which may be the strength we need to walk away from the bar instead of walk into it. An extra half-hour of sleep may take away the time we need to get into the Bible, and so take away the opportunity we need to gain the wisdom in the Scriptures that could help us mend a broken relationship with a friend or family member.

Watching an infomercial? Taking an extra half-hour of sleep? They seem like such small compromises. But when small compromises distract us from the things of God, they can lead to big disasters.

God's Direction, Four Key Decisions, Small Compromises and Big Disasters

There are four key decisions in life that God uses His teachers and His Word to guide us through:

- Choosing a mate and how to develop that relationship.
- Choosing a career and how to develop that career.
- Choosing and maximizing an income level.
- Choosing to walk with God and how to develop that walk.

In this life, God has a marital plan for you, and the devil has a marital plan for you. God has a career path, as does Satan. Both God and the devil have an income level for you. The devil even has a level for your walk with God that he will permit with little interference.

Now, what do you think are the chances that you will make the right choice in each of these key areas without God's direction? No one wants the wrong spouse, the wrong career, or the wrong income level, and if you are wrong in all these areas, you probably will not have a very strong walk with God. However, though we might never intentionally make the wrong choices, we often resist God as He tries to lead us in these areas. For example, we search for our own "teachers" – human, or life examples from secular entertainment, or even well-meaning friends and relatives – who will allow us or encourage us to do what we want, feel what we want, or think what we want. These teachers are found in the world's system of management. They will lead you to make the wrong decisions in many, if not all, of these areas.

Consider Jeff, a young Christian man in his mid-twenties. Relatives introduced him to Ruthann, a very attractive young woman. When they met, Ruthann was beginning her journey to Christ but was yet to be converted. For Jeff and his relatives, it seemed a small compromise for Jeff to begin dating Ruthann. After all, she was so close to meeting Christ as her Savior. As it ended up, Ruthann was the right person for Jeff, but at the wrong time. Each time they were alone (another small compromise), they became just a little more involved physically.

Without a firm conviction against fornication herself, Ruthann couldn't help Jeff overcome sexual temptation. When it came time to "flee youthful lusts" as taught in 2 Timothy 2:22, Ruthann didn't know they *really* needed to and "in the heat of the moment" Jeff didn't want to! Their relationship became marred by sexual immorality – a big disaster. Not long after they fell into that sin, however, Ruthann became a Christian. They changed their behavior to honor both God and Ruthann's newly found faith, and they stayed pure from that point forward. Today Jeff and Ruthann are happily married parents of four children. Even so, Jeff and Ruthann agree that they should have put off dating until Ruthann had soundly converted to faith in Jesus Christ. Then they could have dealt with sexual temptation from the same viewpoint, with the same goals to remain pure.

For Gary, a musician who had been raised in the church, it seemed a small compromise to sing to entertain people in clubs and bars. There was ministry when people enjoyed music anywhere, right? He wouldn't sing anything that was profane or that overtly promoted sin. So what was the problem?

The problem was the club and bar scene assumed a lot about musicians. Bar owners assumed that Gary wanted his hand consistently filled with complimentary drinks. Some sexually active women and men assumed Gary would appreciate nightly invitations to join them in promiscuity. Drug dealers assumed musicians could become some of their best customers, and thought Gary was a likely candidate. He struggled with temptation in all three areas, but finally gave in to a cocaine habit that wiped him out both financially and physically. The process began with a small compromise, and led to a big disaster.

What happens when "good" gets in the way of God's best? Darlene was convinced that she would never be more than a convenience store clerk, although her mentors at church saw she could make a great elementary school teacher. Darlene simply had a knack with children. She had ways of explaining things that children understood. These were gifts her mentors pointed out time and again, along with the fact that she would make much more as a teacher than as a minimum-wage clerk.

The temptation for Darlene was her desire to settle for a career as a retail clerk. It would be an easy compromise to ignore the teaching gifts God had given her to develop. But Darlene's godly mentors never gave up on her. They kept talking with Darlene about the increased impact she could have for Christ. A teacher's salary would allow Darlene to give much more than she could as a retail clerk. As a teacher, Darlene would also have the opportunity to have a godly influence on many more children.

It took time, but Darlene overcame her desire to compromise the gifts God had placed within her. Today she is a respected teacher in a large Christian school, fully using her gifts to God's glory. (There is nothing wrong with being a faithful, Christian retail clerk, by the way, if that is God's gifting and calling on your life. But if God is leading you to another profession and you don't follow Him there, it's disobedience.)

Then there is Ramon. He is a Christian of many years, but also an inconsistent Christian. He cannot seem to manage the "little" areas of obedient Christian living. Bible study, complete honesty, tithing, and pure speech are just a few examples of problem areas for Ramon. Sometimes Ramon has victory in these areas; sometimes he doesn't. He lives a roller-coaster spiritual life: up and down and up again, then down and up and down again.

Satan would like to keep Ramon on this roller-coaster ride for the rest of Ramon's life. Ramon's small compromises in so many "little" things make his inconsistency evident to anyone watching. Ramon professes faith in Christ, and I believe he is saved, but he is so wishy-washy that Ramon has no real testimony about the power of God to change lives – starting with his own. That's a big disaster for the people Ramon could influence.

I believe that if Ramon stopped making small compromises and became faithful in the small things, some big changes would happen for him and the people around him.

Compromise and the Flesh

Romans 8:8 says, *So then they that are in the flesh cannot please God.* If you are a Christian, then you cannot be "in the flesh" (Romans 8:9 *But ye are not in the flesh, but in the Spirit, if so be that the Spirit of God dwell in you*). If you are not saved, your life is lived "in the flesh." However, a Christian is "in Christ"—not in the flesh. Thus we are led of the Spirit, but if your soul [mind, will, and emotions] chooses to take repeated steps [walk] after the prompting of your body, you will find yourself walking "after the flesh." (Romans 8:1b *walk not after the flesh, but after the Spirit.*) This will not please God. Being in the flesh as a non-believer does not please God and walking after the flesh as a believer will displease Him, as well.

We have taught you in previous chapters that your flesh is defined as your soul [mind, will, and emotions] being in subjection to your body [your members]. Living after the flesh is when what you want, feel, or think suppresses what God wants, feels, or thinks. When this takes place, your outer man [the flesh] is overruling your inner man [where the Holy Spirit resides]. You are in control of your life, rather than God. In this case, *you are compromising the work God wants to do in and through you.*

There are many Christian people that think they are pleasing God with their lives. These are well-meaning people. They read their Bibles, go to church, serve in ministries, give sacrificially and share their faith but they are walking after the flesh. They are "after the flesh" because they are doing these things the way *they* want to do them, or the way *they* think they should do them, or the way *they* feel that they should be done. Sure, they are doing good, but they are doing good "after the flesh." Their mind, will, and emotions are not in subjection to God's mind, will and emotions. The soul in us is not yielding to the Spirit. The inner man [the Holy Spirit] is not ruling the body. It is compromised by the lust of the flesh. That is oftentimes described as wicked behavior, but the truth of the matter is that the lust of the flesh is simply defined as the desire of your soul to follow your body's desires, albeit in rebellion to the Holy Spirit.

We that struggle with this are trying hard to do good, but we fail to please God and we do not experience the joy of the Christian life. Why? Because good flesh is just as bad as bad flesh and we cannot please God when we are walking after our flesh, no matter how much good we are doing.

Enduring Without Compromise

In 2 Timothy, Paul tells his trained man who has been called into service to put up with affliction and not be entangled with the concerns [affairs] of this world. Let's look at some other parts of the letter that Paul sent to soldier Timothy to encourage him in his battle with affliction:

> **2 Timothy 2:10** *Therefore I endure all things for the elect's sakes, that they may also obtain the salvation which is in Christ Jesus with eternal glory.*

2 Timothy 1:8 *Be not thou therefore ashamed of the testimony of our Lord, nor of me his prisoner: but be thou partaker of the afflictions of the gospel according to the power of God.*

2 Timothy 3:11 *Persecutions, afflictions, which came unto me at Antioch, at Iconium, at Lystra; what persecutions I endured: but out of them all the Lord delivered me.*

2 Timothy 4:5 *But watch thou in all things, endure afflictions, do the work of an evangelist, make full proof of thy ministry.*

It is clear to me that Paul was anticipating great affliction for young Timothy. He was warning him to not be distracted by the affairs or concerns of this life. He encouraged Timothy to endure without compromise.

I cannot imagine what the affairs of life were like back then. With the persecution of the church, it must have been very grave in comparison to the concerns of our lives today. These days, our main focus tends to be on paying bills, providing for and nurturing our families, personal time, and preparing for retirement. Although this list may not perfectly apply to all people, I have heard all of these "concerns" given as primary reasons why people compromise their faith and fail to serve the God who has called them into service. When we focus on these concerns, we are bad soldiers.

Bad soldiers do not protect the investment of their leader and do not advance upon and free captives from the enemy. In battle, bad soldiers are easily wounded, adversely affecting the entire army. Other soldiers must be made available to meet the medical [in this case, the spiritual] needs of the wounded soldiers, slowing down the advance of that particular infantry division.

Paul is letting Timothy know that the afflictions that he will face as a servant of our Lord Jesus Christ will be manifested as attacks on his personal concerns in life. Those attacks will tempt us to compromise. If we let them, they will weaken our focus on Jesus. But, Paul explains, since we have been called into God's eternal service, we must not focus on temporal matters. Such concerns will certainly be attacked, and we must endure that affliction. If we do not entangle ourselves with those concerns during these attacks, then we will be good soldiers. We will protect our Leader's investments and advance upon the enemy's territory, taking captives for the cause of Christ.

You know, I have found this to be true: whenever my personal life is attacked and I keep my focus on the battle at hand while leaving my own needs in the hands of my Commanding Officer, victory is always just over the hilltop! Yes, we know that we must remain good stewards, and a degree of focus is necessary in our personal and professional lives to maintain good stewardship. However, there is a big difference between focusing on and entangling in the affairs of this life. Defined, we should have "times of concentration" but not "distract ourselves with the concerns of living."

Listen and Cooperate Against Compromise

Preparing yourself to stand against compromise doesn't mean talking more or talking louder. Rather, you must train yourself to listen better.

Mark 4:23-25 is an exciting passage of Scripture:

> *If any man have ears to hear, let him hear. And he said unto them, Take heed what ye hear: with what measure ye mete, it shall be measured to you: and unto you that hear shall more be given. For he that hath, to him shall be given: and he that hath not [he that is not willing to have ears to hear], from him shall be taken even that which he hath.*

These verses speak of cooperation. If we will learn to increase our listening, we will learn how to increase our cooperation. Let's do a little dissecting and defining.

- *Take heed* means "to take notice." He tells us to take notice of what we hear.
- *Measure* means "to ascertain a quantity," as does *mete.*

It's like saying, "with what measure you measure, it shall be measured to you." For example, if you were to walk up to a drinking fountain with a coffee cup, you will be measured a quantity of water that is equal to the measure that you brought to quantify it. You brought a cup; you'll get a cup. Likewise, if you brought a bucket, you will be measured a lot more because you measured using an instrument that had a greater ability to quantify. You can get more if you have a bigger measuring device!

These verses tell us that the more we are prepared to listen, the more we will receive. If we will listen, and listen in abundance, we will be given more things to hear. God will encourage us against compromise. As we listen, we will learn. If we do not listen, we will forget even what we have previously learned.

This is a great example of the proper way in which to cooperate with God. The devil's goal in the life of the unbeliever is to get the soul to lead the body—to walk "after the flesh." To do this, he needs to get us away from the Spirit's leading. He wants us to be uncooperative with God and His system of management. He will do anything within his means to tempt us into compromise. Remember, even a small compromise is a major victory for the devil because it will lead to bigger compromises.

To gain that victory, the devil will oppress to suppress. He will oppress until we are uncooperative with the inner man, and he will suppress us from hearing God's voice of reproof. This will lead to our eventual destruction. But God says to listen to His voice. In fact, increase the quantity in which we are listening. Take advantage of every opportunity to hear. **Do not compromise your opportunities to listen to God:** Bible reading, studying, memorization and meditation, Sunday School, morning service, evening service, mid-week service, preaching tapes, and Christian literature. All of these and many more ways of listening will develop our sensitivity to the inner man and increase our ability to hear and cooperate.

Coaches Against Compromise

No one ever taught me these things as I was growing up. I was raised under God-ordained leadership. They tried to lead me, but I refused their instruction as a teenager and searched for alternate teachers who would allow (and even encourage) me to compromise. All of God's teachers are on the same page, so I had to find teachers that would teach from a different book, so to speak. I found them in the world's system. Teachers who would promote my feelings over God's feelings, my desires over God's desires, my thinking over God's thinking. I found these teachers of ungodly counsel in worldly people, wrong entertainment [bad music and movies], and people who were critical of God's system in an effort to discount its importance to my life. These teachers led me into the ditch that I had to climb out of ten years later. Truthfully, I had to go to the ditch to find them! The result was ten years of loneliness, a horrible résumé, crippling debt, and a separated walk away from God.

But then, while still in that ditch, I came to the realization that in order to build a life that will withstand adversity, I needed to change my direction. I had to refuse even small compromises. Praise God! He picked me up out of that horrible pit and placed my feet upon a solid foundation – the Rock, Christ Jesus – and He established my goings (Psalm 40:2).

How did He establish my goings? He placed me back under God-ordained leadership: people who love God, avoid worldliness, and are positive and uplifting. These people – my preacher, teachers, my parents, my employer, and, yes, even the government – began to lead my life. I followed my preacher's advice, I learned from my teachers, I began to develop my relationship with my parents again, and I worked hard for my employer (as unto Christ) while obeying the laws of the land. **All these people encouraged me to refuse even small compromises as I followed Jesus Christ.** They coached me against compromise.

Everything changed and, for me, it changed quickly. God gave me a beautiful wife within one year. By the second year, He granted me a great career, despite my poor résumé. This career position offered me a rather large income level, and He matched it with a heart to give to others. It wasn't long before I was debt free! Most importantly, He also taught me that I was created to walk with Him, and our relationship with each other began to grow again. What is the cost of following the blind? For me it was a decade of my life, and more.

You need not pay that price. Avoid even the small compromises. Be faithful in the "little things," and God will increase your faithfulness in the big things.

Those Who Do Not Love the Lord Will Not Help Us Serve the Lord.

If ye were of the world, the world would love his own: but because ye are not of the world, but I have chosen you out of the world, therefore the world hateth you.

—John 15:19

Will my friends want anything to do with me now that I am a Christian? That was the question I asked after I gave my life to Jesus. It wasn't long before I found the answer: if I acted like them, they would accept me. When I acted like Christ, they would reject me.

I struggled to determine the correct path. You see, I wanted Christ in my life but I also wanted Christ in my friends' lives. If I broke my ties with my worldly friends, they would lose their opportunity to learn of Christ. So I tried to live as a child of God while hanging out with the devil's kids. As you would expect, more often than not, they would tempt me to do the things that I did not want to do anymore. Eventually, I would give in.

It was at this time God showed me why misery loves company. You see, if I lived right and remained right, my old friends would feel guilt and shame for their behavior. But if I lived wrong, they would prove that Christ has no affect on a person's life. The guilt for their lifestyle would be removed. They would lay the snare [temptation] and wait for me to fall. Proverbs 24:15 says, *Lay not wait, O wicked man, against the dwelling of the righteous; spoil not his resting place* They would work hard to lure me back into the world. They wanted to see that the Christian life doesn't work!

I found that when I got right and stayed right that they went left. However, when the law of sowing and reaping would kick in and they found themselves at the bottom, they would not look to their friends who did the things they did. Rather, they called on me. They would ask me what I did to change my life because my change was real.

What a blessing! I have been able to counsel with literally dozens of friends from the past, in God's timing, and tell them that Christ died for their sins. It has also led to prosperity in my Christian life and blessed happiness. Just like the Bible promises in Psalm 1:1-3 *Blessed* [happy] *is the man that walketh not in the counsel of the ungodly, nor standeth in the way of sinners, nor sitteth in the seat of the scornful* [listens to critical people]. *But his delight is in the law of the LORD; and in his law doth he meditate day and night. And he shall be like a tree planted by the rivers of water, that bringeth forth his fruit in his season; his leaf also shall not wither; and whatsoever he doeth shall prosper.*

Whom Will You Follow?

Whom we follow determines our destination. Luke 6:39-40 says *...Can the blind lead the blind?* [a rhetorical question that sets the stage for Christ's teaching on follow-ship] *shall they not both fall into the ditch? The disciple* [student who follows] *is not above his master* [teacher]: *but every one that is perfect* [properly trained] *shall be as his master* [teacher]. So, we as the followers are not above our teachers. But if we continue to be properly trained, we will be as our teachers. We will become like those whom we follow.

Choosing whom you will follow is very important. Following the wrong person will lead to destruction. Many times in secular programs, people are encouraged to "buddy up" with another person who has the same struggles and addictions. It is meant to be a support for both people. Yet for a Christian with addictions, there are two major flaws with that sort of a system. First, the other person may not have a love for the Lord Jesus Christ in his heart and life. He would not have the same goals, nor even be headed in the same direction, as the Christian should. Second, as our key verse asks, *Can the blind lead the blind? shall they not both fall into the ditch?* It is foolish to follow one who has the same "blindness" as one's self. No victory will be gained when following someone who is struggling in the same area. That person is just as blind. The result of a blind man leading the blind? They *both* will fall.

Psalm 1:1 describes for us the type of people after which we should not be following. *Blessed* [happy] *is the man that walketh not in the counsel of the ungodly* [does not get advice from those who do not love God], *nor standeth in the way of sinners* [does not engage in entertainment with those who do wrong], *nor sitteth in the seat of the scornful* [does not assume the position of critical people]. We will be happy if we choose to *not* follow after the counsel of the ungodly, if we choose to *not* spend time around the worldly systems of entertainment, and if we choose to *not* be influenced by negative people.

Obviously, the best type of people to follow, the best teachers you could choose, are teachers who love God and give counsel as such. These are people who are not worldly in their lifestyles. They will encourage, build up, and edify you and others.

As we discussed in the previous principle, everyone chooses teachers. You are a product of the teachers that you have chosen to follow. God has created a system and the world has created its own system. I call them both systems of management. God's system of management requires those whom He chooses for you to follow to help you make wise decisions. The world, under the authority of its prince, the devil, has a system of management which requires those whom you follow to help you make decisions in your life that *seem* right, but in reality are unwise.

I call God's system of management "The Umbrella of Protection." I call the world's system "The Weathering of Destruction." God's system is intended to protect you from the elements of the world. In contrast, the world's system is intended to destroy you by slowly exposing you to its elements, thus weathering or wearing you down. God's umbrella of protection is His management system for the constant development of our lives. This umbrella consists of those whom He has placed in authority over us: our parents (especially as we are developing into young adults), our preachers, our teachers, our employers, and yes, even the government. These people are God-ordained authorities, designed by God to help us make the right decisions in the development of our lives. They are those God intends for us to follow. In short, they are what the Bible calls teachers or instructors.

Our key verse refers to them by using the Old English word "masters." In the Bible, the word "*master*" is used sometimes to define our employers, sometimes to define our Lord, and sometimes to define our government. In each case, it is referring to the primary function of teaching us. That is what our authorities do: they teach us. If you choose to follow God's ordained authorities, He can work through them to help you make the many wise decisions you will need to make in life. As a matter of fact, even if your authority is not godly, He will still use that person to help mold you. This is not true, however, if you are not under His umbrella of protection. If you choose teachers that are not God-ordained, then you will be exposed to a system that will lead to your eventual destruction. Even if these authorities are good people, your development will be hindered because God has not chosen them to be the authorities through whom He intends to work. Our key verse refers to them as being *blind*. It indicates lack of direction, especially in areas of spiritual direction. Good people without direction from God are blind. They cannot see afar off (2 Peter 1:9). Our verses tell us simply that if we follow those who do not have direction from God, both parties will fall.

What is God's purpose of ordained authority? Why do we need protection from the world's elements? Why is it so important to follow this authority? These are all very good questions. God designs His teachers to instruct us in principles that, when followed, will produce the structure necessary for us to make good decisions. In contrast to teachers who do not love God and so will not help us serve God, God's teachers help us make the most out of opportunities to serve Him.

Leading Others in God's Way

I personally want to spend my time yielding to what God wants me to do, have, and be. But, I have found that when I spend too much time with people of selfish motives, I tend to become somewhat fleshly led to do what I want, to have what I want, and to be what I want. I eventually end up in a very disconcerting position. I do what God wants, but I do it my way; I have what God wants, but I have it my way; I am what God wants, but I am in my own way. I begin to focus on living God's life for me, my way. That is a completely frustrating position to be in, and it comes complete with a loss of joy. Therefore, without isolating myself from my old friends, I am careful to limit my fellowship with them, knowing that *bad company corrupts good morals.*

Some may say that I am wrong for keeping in contact with old friends or for building friendships with people who are not saved. Please realize that the reason I keep a short distance from them is not because I do not love them; rather, it is because I do love them. For surely, when they realize their personal lives need repair, I am often the fortunate one to re-introduce them to Christ at just the right time.

I would ask those who stay closely involved with their unsaved friends, how many have you been able to lead to the Lord? Probably not too many. I have personally experienced the privilege of leading dozens of my old friends to Christ after separating my walk from them, in love. Through diligent prayer, occasional phone calls, letters, cards, and even a few cups of coffee coupled with God's basic law of sowing and reaping, they have returned my outreach by reaching out to me during their times of urgent need. Without fail, each of those friends told me that when they reached their breaking point, I was the only one that they thought could help me. I now enjoy close friendships again with Jeff, Todd, Tom, Tim, Ron, Mike, Darren, Rick, Craig, and even my own brother, Barry!

In my early walk with the Lord, when I tried to balance my relationships with these very same people and others who, at the time, loved the things of the world, their influence on me derailed the Lord's work in my life. He could not clearly direct me because I was directing myself. As I separated from them, God led me on the right path to be what He wanted, to do what He wanted, and to have what He wanted. It has been an incredible joy to experience His desires for my life over my own desires. I dare say that my old friends, who are now my new friends in Christ, are thankful that I made this decision. If you love your friends who do not love God or serve Him, then you will separate – not sever – from them and let the Lord lead them to you when their hearts are the most tender to His call.

The Difference That Friends Make

Additionally, the Holy Spirit will influence us and order our steps through our good Christian friends. Many tend to think that the primary function of Christian friends is merely for socializing or fellowship. But Christian friends are also intended by God to be Spirit-led counselors in our lives. Not all Christians will fit into this category. Proverbs 11:14 says, *in the multitude of counsellors there is safety.* Our multitude of counselors ought to consist of spiritually discerning Christians. Many consider only their pastors as effective counselors for the Lord, but that is not necessarily true. God did not intend for us each to have a multitude of pastors, but He does instruct us to value a multitude of wise counsel. Good Christian friends may help us understand things about God that we do not understand. They may know God better than we know Him in one or more areas.

I think having Christian friends is a must to give the Lord every option in ordering our steps. He wants to work through clean vessels – wise counsel from godly friends. However, if we do not separate from our friends who love the things of this world, we will not have time nor even see the need to make Christian friends. This will hinder God's direction in our lives. Bad friends will consume the time that God intends for us and our good friends to enjoy. Without good Christian friends, we close off one clear channel of communication with the Lord.

We see this explained in part in 2 Corinthians 6:14, 17-18 where we read:

> *Be ye not unequally yoked together with unbelievers: for what fellowship hath righteousness with unrighteousness? and what communion hath light with darkness? Wherefore come out from among them, and be ye separate, saith the Lord, and touch not the unclean thing; and I will receive you. And will be a Father unto you, and ye shall be my sons and daughters, saith the Lord Almighty.*

The picture being drawn here in verse 14 is like that of yoked oxen. Two yoked oxen going in the same direction will produce a desired effect. However, yoking an ox with a horse, or an ox with a lion, would be an unequal yoke. Similarly, we cannot yoke a believer with an unbeliever. Why? They are going in two separate directions.

As believers, we are yoked with Christ. The word *yoke* literally means "to partner." The verse also uses the synonyms *fellowship* and *communion,* which mean the same thing: to partner. Paul is telling us that we should not partner with anyone who has not partnered with Christ. Jesus partners with those whom He lives in and through, and He begins that partnership at the moment they believe. His only *partnership* is with those who believe! If He will not yoke with an unbeliever, then neither should we.

Make no mistake; Paul is not saying that unsaved people are second class nor that they should be avoided. A basic study of the definitions of *friend* and *yoke* will explain the boundaries of our relationship with unbelievers. Truly, there are many options for developing relationships with people that do not require us to yoke with them, or to become partners with them. What God is requesting of us is a separation which is intended to *improve* His work through us that we might reach our lost friends for Him. To be effective for God requires a separated walk. If we want to walk with God, we cannot walk with the world.

An equally explosive topic within the body of Christ is our friendships with other believers. Sometimes these friendships can also greatly hinder our walk with God. We see this admonition found in Romans 16:17-18:

> *Now I beseech you, brethren* [fellow Christians], *mark* [make note of] *them which cause divisions and offences contrary to the doctrine* [right teaching] *which ye have learned; and avoid them. For they that are such serve not our Lord Jesus Christ, but their*

own belly [fleshly appetites]; *and by good words and fair speeches* [creative methods] *deceive the hearts of the simple* [naive].

In these verses, we see some direction given by Paul that is often misunderstood. He is referring to people who claim to love God but do not serve God. Notice, I did not call them Christians. They could be, but they might not be, as well. As Paul tells us, they serve something other than Jesus. They cause divisions and offenses among Christians, especially new believers. Now, I understand that we do not have to see eye to eye on every doctrine to be Christians. However, don't forget in which book of the Bible this verse is found: Romans, the book that contains the road map to heaven. There are many other doctrines found in Romans besides the doctrine of salvation (by grace, through faith), but it is the primary doctrine that is being taught throughout the book of Romans. Obviously, those who reject and cause divisions among people in the doctrine of salvation are unbelievers and must be avoided.

The Test of True Christian Friends: Obedience to the Lord

All believers, especially new believers, must protect themselves from so-called followers of Christ who are not believers in Christ.

Friends should care about your spiritual condition; enemies do not. If you have friends that do not care about your spiritual condition, you need to find new friends. Even when we think we have good friends, they can still do things to harm our spiritual development. Jesus, who was perfect, still had friends who brought him harm. Notice this truth concerning Jesus' friend Judas found in Matthew 26:48-50.

> *Now he that betrayed him gave them a sign, saying, Whomsoever I shall kiss, that same is he: hold him fast. And forthwith he came to Jesus, and*

said, Hail, master; and kissed him. And Jesus said
unto him, Friend, wherefore art thou come? Then
came they, and laid hands on Jesus, and took him.
(Matthew 26:48-50)

Judas appeared to look to Jesus as his teacher, his master. They were friends, but still he doubted Christ's plan for him and did what he deemed was best for himself, not Jesus! Your friends need to believe the things you believe. If they doubt your doctrine, the devil might use them, like he did with Judas, to try to get you to doubt God's plan for you.

There are many who claim to follow Christ and may seek to befriend you. They may even have what appears to be great knowledge about God and power with God. Remember that having apparent spiritual gifts does not necessarily make someone the right type of person to befriend. Matthew 7:22-23 tells of people who had a great degree of spiritual power; I would imagine they would have appeared to be very good Christians, but they were not even saved:

Many will say to me in that day, Lord, Lord, have
we not prophesied in thy name? and in thy name have
cast out devils? and in thy name done many wonder-
ful works? And then will I profess unto them, I never
knew you: depart from me, ye that work iniquity.

Great power? Yes! But power with God? No! Wonderful works? No doubt! But wonderful relationship? Not even close! God says that He never even knew them. The word *knew* means "personal," such as *personal property.* In essence He is saying, "Depart from Me because you were not My personal property." They called Him "Lord." They preached and did miracles in His name, not the name of false gods. In fact, they performed many wonderful works. Good people? Maybe so. But not Christians—and they would be even worse friends! Make sure your friends believe what you believe and make sure they are followers of our Lord.

A key question to ask ourselves when picking our Christian friends is what type of followers are they? The man in our key verse was a follower of Jesus, but he was also a tempter of Jesus. Judas was a follower of Jesus, but he was also a betrayer of Jesus. The false prophets and miracle workers in Matthew 7 were followers of Jesus, but not believers in Jesus.

You see, a true follower is known by obedience. Jesus said in Luke 6:46, *And why call ye me, Lord, Lord, and do not the things which I say?* Wow! What a convicting verse! We call Him "Lord, Lord" (which is what the unsaved people called Him in Matthew 7) and yet we do not obey Him. Jesus told us that His sheep follow what He tells them. In John 10:26-27 He said, *But ye believe not, because ye are not of my sheep, as I said unto you. My sheep hear my voice, and I know them, and they follow me.* He not only speaks to His sheep, but His sheep follow His spoken word. What is the key ingredient to being His sheep? Believing in Him. He goes on to say, "I know them." Oh, how glad I am that He will not say to me one day, "I never knew you," but rather will say, "I know him." Why? Because I believed. After that, I made a conscious choice to exercise my belief by following His word, spoken and written. I became obedient. You must do this to become victorious over stubborn habits; and *you must surround yourself with others who will do this, as well.*

Psalm 1: Getting the Right Advice from the Right People

The formula for happiness is in Psalm 1:1-3. It is 100 percent dependent upon whom we allow to influence us. Let's take a look at this familiar passage and then dissect and define it so that we can understand it better

> *Blessed is the man that walketh not in the counsel of the ungodly, nor standeth in the way of sinners, nor sitteth in the seat of the scornful. But his delight is*

in the law of the LORD; and in his law doth he meditate day and night. And he shall be like a tree planted by the rivers of water, that bringeth forth his fruit in his season; his leaf also shall not wither; and whatsoever he doeth shall prosper.

Blessed is an old English word for the Modern English word *happy*. Thus, this is the formula for being happy. It involves three don'ts and three dos. Let's look at the three don'ts:

Don't #1: Don't walk in the counsel of the ungodly. Don't get advice from those who do not love God. In other words, don't allow ungodly people to influence you.

Don't #2: Don't stand in the way of sinners. Don't fellowship with people whose course in life will introduce you to sin. People who engage in sinful habits should be avoided. In other words, you don't allow sinful people to influence you!

Don't #3: Don't sit in the seat of the scornful. Don't take the position of those who are critical of others. In other words, you don't allow critical people to influence you!

Then the three dos:

Do #1: Delight in God's law. This requires developing an appetite. The three don'ts will suppress your appetite for God's word. The more you eat the greater your appetite.

Do #2: Meditate on the law all day. This requires a form of memorization that will allow you to be influenced by the inner man throughout the day with the verses you have memorized.

Do #3: Meditate on the law all night. This requires us to not only use His Word to help us out in our workplace, but also in our homes (or vice versa if you work nights). Such a person does not cease to be influenced by his inner man just because he is in the comfort of his own home.

To put it all together, the formula for happiness in the Christian life (despite our curse of sorrow) is avoiding the negative influence of ungodly, sinful, and critical people, plus devouring God's Word to the point of memorization so the inner man may be a positive influence all day and all night.

Happiness is found in influence. Not who you are influencing, but rather Who is influencing you through His Word and the people He uses.

Our Sinful Habits Do Hurt Those Who Follow Us.

For none of us liveth to himself, and no man dieth to himself.

—Romans 14:7

Have you ever wondered if anybody cared about you? Have you ever thought about trying something drastic to get yourself noticed?

One of the lies from the father of lies [the devil] is that no one cares about us, no one is watching us, so no one is affected by our behavior. Since the dawn of time, Satan has deceived us into believing that our behavior will only affect, hurt, or damage ourselves.

- Satan deceived Eve in the very beginning. Little did she know that her sin would then be shared by her husband, which in turn would lead to the fall of man and woman. Little did she know that God would place a curse her and her husband—and all generations to follow. The devil also deceived Lot. Not realizing that day-to-day contact with sinners would damage his family, Lot reluctantly left his homeland. His lack of leadership in his family led to his wife's death, his daughters' out-of-control behavior, and his own sinful choices. The devil deceived David. Little did the king know that if he stayed home from battle (where he should have been at the time), he would face a temptation that would lead him into adultery. As a consequence, that woman's husband would be murdered in a a scheme developed by David himself, and her newborn son would die.

Over and over again in Scripture we see that sinful behavior has a profound effect on those who follow us. Who, then, are the people who follow you? Those people who are in relationship with yours. If you were to die today, would one hundred people be at your funeral? Most people would like to think so. How about fifty? Or thirty-five? Or twenty? How about one? Would at least one person be at your funeral? Yes, I believe we would all have at least one person at our funeral, and probably closer to one hundred. Well, those are the people that your behavior hurts. Those are the people affected by your sinful habits. They may not feel the same pain you feel, but they feel pain. They may not say the things to you that would help you, but they think them and wish they could find the courage to say them.

Romans 14:7 says, *None of us liveth to himself, and no man dieth to himself.* Your life affects other people the same way your death will. So choose today to let your life have a profoundly positive effect on others. No matter the cost, no matter the sacrifice, make that choice.

Without a doubt, the best leader for any of us to follow is Jesus Christ. We also do well to follow the best *forms* of Christ, those authorities He has ordained to serve. If we allow those godly people to teach us, if we will submit to their leading and direction in life, then we will become fully informed and someday be teachers and examples to those around us. As 2 Timothy 2:2 says, *The things that thou hast heard of me among many witnesses, the same commit thou to faithful men, who shall be able to teach others also.*

For better or worse, our lives become textbooks to those people we influence and lead. We must be very aware of whether our example helps them or hurts them

A Flawed Focus

Our real problem in hurting those who follow us begins with a flaw in our focus. Hear what Jesus taught in Luke 6:41-42:

> *Why beholdest thou the mote that is in thy brother's eye, but perceivest not the beam that is in thine own eye? Either how canst thou say to thy brother, Brother, let me pull out the mote that is in thine eye, when thou thyself beholdest not the beam that is in thine own eye? Thou hypocrite, cast out first the beam out of thine own eye, and then shalt thou see clearly to pull out the mote that is in thy brother's eye.*

In these verses, Jesus talked about the focus of our life, about what we fix our attention on. Jesus explained a flaw in that focus, a flaw we all tend to have at times. To be specific, we focus on the perceived spiritual needs and weaknesses of others rather than on our own spiritual needs and weaknesses. A mote is a small particle, and a beam is a large piece of lumber. Though somewhat humorous, this illustration effectively shows how flawed our focus can be. Jesus described a Christian who was trying to assist another Christian with a flaw. The helper asks permission to help, explaining, "You have a small particle in your eye." The helper does not even realize that he should be focusing on the large obstruction in his own eye, an obstruction that hinders his ability to help anyone else. Jesus called that person a hypocrite, and in the Greek *hypocrite* means "actor." So Jesus was saying, "You actor! You must first handle your own large sin problems before you can begin to understand how to help others deal with their smaller sin problems."

In this parable, our Lord taught that we cannot see clearly how to help someone who has a small problem until we first understand we have a large problem and then find someone to help you rectify it. Only then are we qualified to help our brothers. Our focus should always begin on our own personal weaknesses and flaws.

But it's always easier—infinitely easier—to look at other people's flaws rather than our own. Romans 2:21 reads, *Thou therefore which teachest another, teachest thou not thyself? thou that preachest a man should not steal, dost thou steal?* The "people" mentioned here are teachers and preachers, yet they do not follow their own advice. I believe Paul admonished teachers and preachers because they themselves sometimes focus on the needs of others, forgetting to address on their own sins and needs. Just as our God-ordained authority figures can sometimes focus on others rather than on themselves and their own sinful ways, so can you and I who are a couple of their followers.

Romans 2:24 goes on to say, *For the name of God is blasphemed among the Gentiles through you, as it is written.* The word *blasphemed* means "to speak evil of." The Bible is saying that unbelievers speak evil of God as a result of the hypocrisy of some teachers and preachers. When our flaws are obvious to those we are seeking to help, we cannot see clearly enough to help them, and those who are watching us realize we are just actors, or hypocrites. Our hypocrisy makes God look bad.

Proverbs 20:6 reminds us, *Most men will proclaim every one his own goodness: but a faithful man who can find?* Most people are able to share how good they are when they speak to others (they are talkers), but to follow that proclamation with a faithfulness that proves their faith (a walker) is quite difficult. Verse 7 goes on to say, *The just man walketh in his integrity: his children are blessed after him.* There are lots of talkers, but very few walkers. I don't know about you, but I want to be a walker *and* a talker. I want God to develop me in such a way that I am qualified to teach and lead others. As a matter of fact, if you are a walker and not merely a talker, your offspring [physical and spiritual] will be happy because of it. Your integrity directly affects the level of contentment of those following you.

Now hear a story Jesus told in Luke 18:10-14:

> *Two men [who] went up into the temple to pray; the one a Pharisee [a law-abiding sect of the Jews], and the other a publican [a tax collector]. The Pharisee stood and prayed thus with himself, God, I thank thee, that I am not as other men are, extortioners, unjust, adulterers, or even as this publican. I fast twice in the week, I give tithes of all that I possess.*

Notice that the Pharisee lists for God all that he doesn't do wrong and all that he does right. But he makes no mention of what he does wrong! Consider this contrast:

> *The publican, standing afar off, would not lift up so much as his eyes unto heaven, but smote upon his breast, saying, God be merciful to me a sinner. [Jesus said]. I tell you, this man went down to his house justified rather than the other.*

The word *justify* here does not mean "saved." It means "conformed to the law." This "sinner" was more conformed to the law than the teacher of the law because his focus was on what he did that was wrong rather than on what he did that was right or what others did that was wrong. Jesus went on to teach that *for every one that exalteth himself shall be abased; and he that humbleth himself shall be exalted.* (Boy, ain't that the truth!)

Do you remember the Old Testament account of David and Bathsheba? What a sad example of overlooking our flaws and judging the flaws of another. Read 2 Samuel 12:1-7 here:

> *The LORD sent Nathan unto David...and said unto him, There were two men in one city; the one rich, and the other poor. The rich man had exceeding many flocks...the poor man had nothing, save one little ewe lamb, which he had bought and nourished up...and was unto him as a daughter. And there came a traveller unto the rich man, and he...took the poor man's lamb, and dressed it for the man that was come to him. And David's anger was greatly kindled against the man; and he said to Nathan, As the LORD liveth, the man that hath done this thing shall surely die... and Nathan said to David, Thou art the man.*

The beam in David's eye was large, yet he didn't even notice it when faced with the flaw of another. David was a hypocrite; he was an actor. He believed that the rich man should die for his selfish act of theft, but he didn't see anything wrong with his own theft and the murder of the person from whom he had stolen. David's focus was off. Way off. And it cost him dearly. But to his credit, the lessons he learned from this failed focus changed his life for the better...forever (see Psalm 51).

John 8:3-11 offers another illustration of religious leaders focusing on the shortcomings of others:

> *The scribes and Pharisees brought unto him [Jesus] a woman taken in adultery; and when they had set her in the midst, They say unto him, Master, this woman was taken in adultery, in the very act. Now Moses in the law commanded us, that such should be stoned: but what sayest thou?... [Jesus] lifted up himself, and said unto them, He that is without sin among you, let him first cast a stone at her... And they which heard it, being convicted by their own conscience, went out one by one... and Jesus was left alone, and the woman standing in the midst. When Jesus had lifted up himself, and saw none but the woman, he said unto her, Woman, where are those thine accusers? hath no man condemned thee? She said, No man, Lord. And Jesus said unto her, Neither do I condemn thee: go, and sin no more.*

What hypocrisy! These scribes and Pharisees, these religious leaders and teachers, were ready to kill this woman who had sin in her life. Jesus simply reminded them of their own flaws and commented that anyone without a flaw could throw that first stone. Examining their own flaws led these men to be convicted of their own sin—and recognizing our own flaws should have the same effect on us. They walked away from the woman, realizing they were no better than she. Then Jesus, the only flawless man in the crowd, decided rather than to condemn her, to encourage her: *go, and sin no more.* She was fortunate to be alive despite the law of the day, and rather than placing her in bondage and condemnation, Jesus set her free gave her an opportunity to live independent of the power of sin.

What a beautiful picture of what Christ did for us at Calvary! Rather than condemn us, He provided Himself as a sacrifice. That sacrifice not only paid the penalty for our sin and save us from deserved and certain condemnation, but it also provided us emancipation from the power of sin and gave us freedom from the accuser!

We Christians therefore need to be more compassionate and gracious toward those who are struggling. Consider the warning of Galatians 6:1: *Brethren, if a man be overtaken in a fault, ye which are spiritual, restore such an one in the spirit of meekness; considering thyself, lest thou also be tempted. Meekness* is "getting along with others without causing friction." *Spiritual* means "consisting of a Spirit." Before Christ, your spirit is dead; after Christ, your spirit is "made alive," and His Spirit comes to dwell within you. Though we may not act like it at times, we are referred to in the Bible as being spiritual or "consisting of a living Spirit."

Paul taught that if a brother in Christ has a flaw, fellow Christians should *restosre* him. The word restore means "to return to [his] former place." It does not necessarily mean return to his former position of leadership. But he should be returned to his former place, specifically to his relationship that was strained as a result of his flaw. Paul also taught that this should be done with fellow believers in a spirit of meekness, a temperament of cooperation. He warned that if we fail to restore a fellow believer because we our attitude results in division or discord, we ourselves could be tempted. Paul told to consider ourselves and look at our own flaws. Before we tackle another man's faults, we need to look at our own. We need to return ourselves to our former fellowship with Christ, then we will have the right temperament and attitude to help restore others.

If you are like me, you are more comfortable justifying your flaws by comparing them to the flaws of others. Second Corinthians 10:12 says, *For we dare not make ourselves of the number, or compare ourselves with some that commend themselves: but they measuring themselves by themselves, and comparing themselves among themselves, are not wise.* Especially as we lead others, it is very foolish to compare ourselves to anyone other than our Lord Jesus Christ. If we stay focused on His example and let Him be our standard, we will be less inclined to turn a blind eye to our own flaws. Otherwise, our sinful habit of finding flaws in others will wound those we lead.

Fruitful Leadership Points People to New Life in Christ

Fruit means "outcome, or result." Luke 6:43-35 compares a good tree vs. a corrupt tree to a good man vs. an evil man. This comparison is based on their fruit, on the outcome or result of their lives:

> For a good tree bringeth not forth corrupt fruit; neither doth a corrupt tree bring forth good fruit. For every tree is known by his own fruit. For of thorns men do not gather figs, nor of a bramble bush gather they grapes. A good man out of the good treasure of his heart bringeth forth that which is good; and an evil man out of the evil treasure of his heart bringeth forth that which is evil: for of the abundance of the heart his mouth speaketh.

A good man will bring forth that which is good from the good treasure of his heart. We are not talking about a physical heart that pumps blood and sustains life. We are referring to the seat of affections and passions. When your motive is good, the outcome of your actions will be good. Thinking back to the comparison of the man with the beam trying to help the man with the mote, we must understand that Jesus taught that if we are to help other people and see positive results, we must have the right motives.

In our key verses about being fruitful, Jesus spoke of *treasure,* of "a great quantity of a thing that is collected for future use." The majority of the things we store in our seats of affections are for later use. That is, they are stored until our hearts feel they are needed. When we are faced with life's circumstances, our seats of affections and passions will respond. So if we store in our seats of affections self-centered, possession-centered thoughts and we store in our seats of passions thoughts of bitterness, resentment, anger, or malice, then when we are faced with adversity, these passions and affections will feel violated and run rampant. This will be the outcome or result of "the great quantity that we collected for future use." The evil treasure of our hearts brings forth [bears fruit] that which is evil. Jesus went on to say, *For of the abundance* [great quantity or overflow] *of the heart* [the] *mouth speaketh.*

Our verses remind us, however, that this principle works both ways. If we collect for future use an affection for things above (Colossians 3:2) and capture and collect our God-given passion for love, joy, peace, and the other fruits of the Spirit, then when faced with a circumstance that violates those affections and passions, we will respond properly. Just as it is impossible for a good tree to bear bad fruit, so we will bear fruit based on what we have collected in our hearts as treasure.

What fruit does God really want to see in the lives of His people? What does God want the outcome, or result, of your life and mine to be? The answer is found in John 15:8: *Herein is my Father glorified, that ye bear much fruit; so shall ye be my disciples.* Whenever you see the word *herein,* ask yourself, "Why is that word in here?" Look closely at that verse. It gives us the formula for glorifying God with our lives. God is glorified—or made to look good—when we bear much fruit. According to this verse, it is impossible for us to truly be a disciple or student of Christ and not bear much fruit. If your fruit is lacking, you are not the student that Christ wants you to be. Your fruit must not only be good, but it must be much, in great quantity. That is the only way to make God look good. He lists no other thing that glorifies Him "in here." Jesus indicated with the "herein" that you make God look good by bearing much fruit. That fruit makes it clear that you are one of His students who is truly following Him.

And what is the fruit of a Christian? A well-meaning Christian would probably first respond with Galatians 5:22-23—*love, joy, peace, longsuffering, gentleness, goodness, faith, meekness, temperance.* But those are not the fruit of a Christian. Those are the fruit, or result, of the Holy Spirit indwelling a Christian. I believe that Proverbs 11:30 states the outcome, or fruit, of a Christian life: *The fruit of the righteous is a tree of life.*

Stored away in my parents' home is a photo album with a family tree drawn inside. That family tree represents the outcome, or result, of marriage unions from generation to generation. Similarly, our marriage union with Jesus Christ should have obvious outcomes or results. I believe the Bible indicates clearly that the outcome, or result, of our marriage union with Jesus Christ is baby Christians: the offspring of Christ, who gave life, should direct that same opportunity of life to others. You will become fruitful when you, as you become a leader, begin to invest in the eternal destination of other people.

Revelation 22:17 tells us how to direct people to this opportunity of new life: *The Spirit* [the Holy Spirit] a*nd the bride* [the church] *say, Come. And let him that heareth* [that's you!] *say, Come. And let him that is athirst* [the lost] *come. And whosoever will, let him take the water of life freely.* I believe this verse is encouraging us to invite lost people to attend church with us. But let's look at this admonition in reverse. It tells us that if we who have heard and taken of the water of life invite those who are lost and without this life-giving water to "Come [to church]," they will come. The bride [meaning the church and its pastor] along with the Spirit of God [during the invitation], will then say, "Come." If the thirsty come, they will drink of this water and never thirst again (John 4:14). We have a responsibility to beckon others to come and drink of the Water of Life. Doing so glorifies God! Followers of Jesus will bear the fruit of baby Christians.

Obedience to God Eliminates Sinful Habits That Harm Others

Obedience to God is the fundamental element in living the victorious Christian life and therefore a prerequisite for success as Christians. It. Luke 6:46 says, *Why call ye me, Lord, Lord, and do not the things which I say?* How can we call Jesus our Master yet refuse to do what He has told us to do?

God wants to communicate with us. He leads and instructs us through preachers/teachers. He gives wisdom through many counselors. He guides and directs through His Word. He communicates to us in prayer, and He leads and convicts us through His indwelling Spirit. These five forms of communication are intended to help us fulfill His will for our life, and they will help build us into the people God calls us to be.

In John 16:7-14 we see an absolutely incredible truth being explained. As Jesus spoke to His disciples, He said, *Nevertheless I tell you the truth.* [Usually, when someone prefaces a statement with *I am telling you the truth,* I wonder if that person normally tells me lies, but that is not what Jesus meant. Instead He was making the point, "What I am about to tell you is going to be really hard to believe."] *It is expedient* [better] *for you that I go away: for if I go not away, the Comforter will not come unto you; but if I depart, I will send him unto you.*

I know exactly why that would seem so hard to believe. I mean, if Jesus were living beside me and I had been with Him for years, I would definitely think I was better off with Him than I'd be without Him. As a matter of fact, if you look at the lives of the disciples, they probably thought that same thing. I mean, what a bunch of losers! They couldn't seem to do anything right. They often questioned our Savior, and they didn't have the faith to trust Him in many areas. Some disciples were very concerned about who was going to be in charge and who was going to be considered the greatest in the kingdom that Christ was promising to them. These guys were doomed if Christ left. Sure enough, when He was arrested and imprisoned [still on earth in bodily form, but taken from them in presence], the disciples all took off like a bunch of yellow-bellies. Some went back to their old occupations; one even denied that he knew Jesus. Do you see why it would be so hard for the disciples to believe that they would be better off without Him?

However, a short time later Jesus did leave this earth, and after His ascension into heaven, He sent——as promised—His Comforter. What was the result? These eleven yellow-bellied men went on to change the world. Ten of them died horrible martyrs' deaths. History proves that each was given an opportunity to recant his faith, but each one refused.

Now, what in the world happened? How did these losers go from being scared of persecution while Jesus was here to changing the world and dying for His cause after He was gone? What changed them was the fact that they were indwelt with the Holy Spirit. In what ways did the Spirit help them? Let's look further into our verses in John 16:7-14: *Howbeit when he, the Spirit of truth, is come, he will guide you into all truth: for he shall not speak of himself; but whatsoever he shall hear, that shall he speak:* The Spirit of Truth—the Spirit of Jesus—will guide you and me into truth. He will not exalt Himself; He will simply share what He has been instructed by Christ to share. *He will show you things to come* [enlighten us about hidden things]. *He shall glorify me* [the Spirit will make Jesus look good]: *for he shall receive of mine* [the Spirit will take what Jesus gives Him], *and shall show* [reveal] *it unto you.*

Here is the amazing truth. We see in Acts 1:8 that we *shall receive power, after that the Holy Ghost is come upon* [us]. Juxtaposed with the John 16 passage, we see that the Holy Ghost comes *in* us and the Holy Ghost comes *upon* us. You may ask, "So how does this help us live a better life than we would if Jesus were still with us?" Well, the answer to that question is simple to understand but hard to live out because of the enemy's interference and attacks. The answer is that, by the Holy Spirit, Jesus will communicate truth to us through one or more of those five forms of communication mentioned earlier. When God's truth is shared, it will bear witness with the Spirit within us. The Spirit will then guide and direct us, often by convicting us of our failure to obey or live according to that truth. When this happens, we will become uncomfortable. While we are in this uncomfortable position, we can ask God to help us fulfill His request or truth. Then He will often step in and send the Power of the Holy Ghost up and on us and make us *comfortable* doing something that makes us *uncomfortable.* The primary function of the indwelling Holy Spirit is to make us uncomfortable with error in our lives. The primary function of the influence of the Holy Spirit *upon* us is to give us the power to be comfortable with His direction so that we may fulfill the leading of the indwelling Spirit to correct that error. Otherwise, we risk not only our own spiritual well-being, but the spiritual well-being of those who watch us and follow us.

When we say no to the Spirit's conviction of our sin, no to being uncomfortable, then we weaken His Spirit's influence over our human soul?. When we reject the Spirit's leading, we will eventually reject His feeding, and we will stave off the Spirit's ability to communicate to us. We will not listen to our preachers or teachers, we will not seek counsel, we will not read Scripture or try to understand what we read, and our prayers will be nothing more than grocery lists—if we pray at all.

Why does this happen? Because we are unwilling to be uncomfortable. If God had intended for us to be comfortable, for us to never know discomfort, He would not have sent us a Comforter! You will not see God's power on your life or ministry until you allow His Spirit to communicate to you your error and allow yourself to sit with that uncomfortable feeling of conviction that prods you to turn to God with a desire to obey Him fully. When you respond to the Spirit's conviction and repent of your sin, God will step in with Holy Power from on high and make you comfortable again. Remember, if you are serving God and you are comfortable, then you do not need a Comforter. Furthermore, you are serving God in your power, not His. If you are doing anything in your power, then you are walking after the flesh, and your mind is in rebellion to the Spirit as well as in subjection to your own lustful desires. *For they that are after the flesh do mind the things of the flesh; but they that are after the Spirit the things of the Spirit* (Romans 8:5). Don't call Jesus your Lord or Master or Teacher unless you are doing what He has commanded, unless you are fulfilling His requests. Only as we obey can those who watch us and follow us see a God-honoring life pattern that they can safely model their own lives.

Increasing One's Knowledge of God: The Positive Power of Sanctification

Consider the teaching of Colossians 1:10: *Walk worthy of the Lord unto all pleasing, being fruitful in every good work, and increasing in the knowledge of God.*

Knowing God is essential to our sanctification. When we were first saved, we became justified and sanctified. *Sanctified* means "set apart," and we are set apart for God's use. He dwells within us in the form of His Spirit, the Holy Ghost. So we now have His power within us, and—as evidenced in the New Testament—He can use us in miraculous ways. This indwelling of God's Spirit does not mean, however, that we automatically enjoy the benefits of sanctification. Remember, the benefit of justification takes place because God knows you; the benefits of sanctification take place as you know God. You and I must grow in our knowledge of God if we are to experience the benefits of His power in our lives.

You do not, however, need to know power to use power, but you need to know power if you are to be used by power. Let me give you an analogy. You see, power is the ability to use a resource and overcome certain circumstances by doing so. If, for instance, you entered a dark room, your first reaction would be to reach for the power source—the light switch. The light would turn on, and the darkness would be overcome because you used the resource of the electric company's power supply. You used the power, but the power did not use you. But you must realize that the light switch was made available for your use because someone was used by that source of power for your benefit. Let me explain.

In order for the power to be available for you to use, someone had to be used by the power source. In order for that light switch to be there, an electrician was used to place it in that position. Thus, the electric company used him to channel the power into a position where it could be used to overcome darkness. What was the prerequisite for that electrician to be used by the power source? Very simply, he had to understand and know this power. He had to understand how electrical power works. The electrician had to increase his knowledge of this power until he understood how to best use it for his own benefit and for the benefit of others who could then use it themselves. A person must be properly trained in electrical power before he or she works with it. It is that simple.

Second Peter 1:3 says, *According as his divine power hath given unto us all things that pertain unto life and godliness, through the knowledge of him that hath called us to glory and virtue.* The more accurately, the more generally, we know God, the more He will be able to use us in His kingdom work. That is why Colossians 1:10 offers two admonitions for pleasing God: we will please Him if we are bearing fruit from our good efforts, and those good efforts will be fruitful if we increase our knowledge of Him, because He will be the One providing His power for our good efforts. Power with God brings power [influence] with man!

The apostle James spoke of the relationship between faith and works (James 2:14-26). That is faith *plus* effort. When we witness, it is our effort and the other person's faith that lead them to Christ. Bottom line, God does the work of saving: [The gospel of Christ] *is the power of God unto salvation to everyone that believeth* (Romans 1:16). That power is a resource for overcoming a sinful soul's destiny by someone who is being *utilized* by God, not someone who *uses* God, but even more He wants to utilize us. To be used by God, we must know Him, and to know Him is to be used by Him. Christians who are being used by God, rather than simply using God, will bring Him great pleasure. People around us may also benefit when God uses us because they may gain the great benefit of the Power that we point them to by sharing of our faith. In other words, if we are experiencing the benefits of sanctification, then as a result, other people will experience the benefits of justification. We will not hurt them by our sinful habits. Instead, they will benefit from our increasing knowledge of God!

Today and tomorrow and onward from this point, let your good habits help those people who watch and follow you. Choose today to be a faithful learner at church. Choose to read your Bible regularly. Choose to talk to God in prayer. Choose to arm yourself with memorized Bible verses that will help you overcome your biggest battles Choose today to help those who come into your program. Choose today to make a difference in the lives of your congregation, the lives of your community, a difference for the kingdom of God.

It Is Not Possible to Fight a Fleshly Temptation with Fleshly Weapons.

Ye are of God, little children, and have overcome them: because greater is he that is in you, than he that is in the world.

—1 John 4:4

So many times we have lost students either tempo-rarily or permanently because they believed the lie of the devil that the world had something to offer their recovery. Whether it be "the Patch," secular counseling, evaluation of child-hood, methadone, Prozac, or any other fleshly [worldly] weapon that is intended to curb our stubborn habits and inappropriate behavior, it will not cure us of our affliction. Praise God, the battle is inside of us, and that is exactly where Christ has chosen to take up residence in our lives! You see, the battle cannot be won with a fleshly [worldly] weapon because the battle is spiritual.

Second Corinthians 10:3-5 says, *For though we walk in the flesh, we do not war after the flesh: (For the weapons of our warfare are not carnal [fleshly], but mighty through God [spiritual] to the pulling down of strong holds) Casting down imaginations [in your mind], and every high thing that exalteth itself against the knowledge of God, and bringing into captivity every thought to the obedience of Christ.*

It is simple to believe but hard to apply. Whenever we have a stubborn thought, we must cast it down. Remember, as a man thinks in his heart, so is he. Principle #2 says every sin has its origin in our hearts. It is our responsibility to protect our hearts with all diligence because out of the heart are the very most important issues in life. If there is going to be any good or anything worth commending come out of our lives, we must first concentrate on things that are true, honest, just, lovely, pure and of good report (Philippians 4:8). To avoid a habitual action or reaction to our negative thoughts we must cast down the thought and bring our mind under subjection to the obedience of Christ. We will have a lot of help with this, you see, because 1 John 4:4 says, *Ye are of God, little children, and have overcome them: because greater is he that is in you, than he that is in the world.*

The world has nothing to offer you in your quest for recovery. You can believe what you are reading or you can try the world your-self. But with Christ, all things are possible, if you only believe.

Mighty Through God: Overcoming Through Christ

How do you overcome a fleshly temptation? As Galatians 2:20 reminds us, through *the Son of God, who loved me, and gave himself for me.* In fact, God gave Himself for me for this very purpose. Not for me to be me, but for me to overcome through Him by relinquishing self-ownership to God.

If I give $10,000 for a car, I do not give it so the car can have some spending money. I give it so the car will belong to me and take me wherever I want to go. The same is true with Christ's gift: He gave it to take ownership of us. We have given Him our hearts by being reborn, and now we must submit our lives to Him, also. We know that without God's power, we cannot gain freedom in Christ. We have tried to work out our problems, but we just can't do it. The key is to overcome our sinful habits by the power that is within us, the power of the Holy Spirit. Remember, Philippians 4:13 says, *I can do all things through Christ which strengtheneth me.* We must yield our "rights" to Christ and let Him work through us to overcome our sinful habits.

A key verse that explains this truth is found in 1 Corinthians 6:19-20:

> *What? know ye not that your body is the temple of the Holy Ghost which is in you, which ye have of God, and ye are not your own? For ye are bought with a price: therefore glorify God* [make Him look good] *in your body* [your outward actions], *and in your spirit* [your inner man], *which are God's.*

Jesus Christ gave His body to redeem us and His Spirit to guide us. We are His, inside and out! The impetus of this knowledge should be a constant motivation for us to continually make God look good.

Let me warn you that as we relinquish our lives to the Lord and begin to see victories, Satan is going to work that much harder to get us to doubt our abilities to serve God. The devil sees our spiritual growth, also. He will do everything he can to mess up the new path we are trodding – the new seeds we are sowing.

If the devil is not attacking us, then there is something wrong in our lives. Any growth on our part will attract the attention of the devil. He is the Great Deceiver, and he knows how to sneak into our lives. He knows our weak spots. Yet, we need to continually relinquish self-ownership to God to keep the devil from gaining any victory in our lives. If we make a mistake, we can remain confident that God is still going to finish what He started in us. Philippians 1:6 says, *Being confident of this very thing, that he which hath begun a good work in you will perform it until the day of Jesus Christ.* God is going to complete what He began in us!

Let God Do the Work

The key to harmony with God is submission. Start by submitting to God the very idea that you can fight a fleshly temptation with a fleshly weapon, no matter how sophisticated it appears to be. Don't try to make excuses for your struggles. Just determine that if God says something is wrong, it is wrong–submit to Him! That is why we were crucified with Christ. That is why He lives within us. That is why we must exercise our faith in willing submission to His leading. Making God look good makes us look good. You are dead. Nevertheless, you live! To live like Christ, you must act like a dead man.

Throughout this book we have discussed the role of the inner man. The inner man is God in us, looking to live through us to produce power for us, that we might do great exploits for Him. If God is going to be living His life in us, and as a result of our submission, through us, as well, then we ought to be able to determine, by observation, when He is actually leading us and when we are instead leading ourselves.

In retrospect, we have learned that when the outer man is in submission to the body, then we are in the flesh. Even if we are doing good, we are in the flesh because we are doing good in our own power rather than the power of God.

In Galatians 2:21, Paul told the church of Galatia that this type of behavior will frustrate the grace of God. Grace is where God is doing His work. *Frustrate* means "to interrupt." Thus, Paul is charging the church members of Galatia with interrupting God's work on their behalf. How were they doing this? In the third verse of chapter three, Paul writes, *Are ye so foolish? having begun in the Spirit, are ye now made perfect by the flesh?* The church of Galatia, which had been greatly used by God, had ceased to submit to the Spirit's work in their lives and were trying to develop themselves spiritually in their own power. This is an incredibly frustrating place to be. It frustrates us when we live this way because despite our efforts to do good, we are living absent of joy and it frustrates our God that is living in us. Why does this frustrate God? Because He is trying to do a good work, but we will not allow Him to perform it. We are not under the Spirit's control; we are exercising soul control!

In Galatians 5:17-23, we see an explanation of this battle between our flesh and the Spirit of God. Verse 17 begins, *For the flesh lusteth against the Spirit, and the Spirit against the flesh...*This tells us that our soul desires to yield to the body rather than yield to the Spirit's leading. It also tells us that the Spirit wants to lead the soul of man, rather than for the body to lead the soul.

Paul goes on to say, *and these are contrary the one to the other.* He is telling us something that is very obvious. These two desires of the body and the Spirit are contrary, or opposite, of each other. There is no middle ground. The Spirit will lead as the soul submits to Him. If not, we will be ruled by the body, as the soul rebels against the Spirit's leading. This is otherwise known as self-control. Many people think self-control is good, but it's not. It is better than no control, but the only good option is Spirit control. Remember,...*in me* [in my flesh] *dwelleth no good thing...*(Romans 7:18).

The last phrase of Galatians 5:17 gives us the biggest struggle of the Christian life, yet explains it at the very same time. It reads, *ye cannot do the things that ye would.* The biggest struggle of the Christian life is trying to do the things that we would like to be able to do. We want to do the right things and we try to do the right things, but that is our biggest problem. We are trying hard to do good. We also see the reason why this effort is so futile: Paul tells us that we *cannot* do the things that we would. Have you ever seen this before? You cannot do it. You cannot live the Christian life in your own power. Only Christ can live the Christian life. We have to stop trying and let God do the work, especially in the fight against fleshly temptations.

This is grace! Grace is when God does the work; the law is where man does the work. If you are trying to do what you would (or should), you will ultimately fail, and lose your joy, as well! However, if you would let God do what you would like to be able to do, then victory is certain.

Further explanation of this truth is given in the next verse, where Paul tells us, *But if ye be led of the Spirit, ye are not under the law.* If God is leading us and we are following Him in step, then we are walking in the Spirit. We will not be under the law (where we must try to do the work, yet where we cannot do the work), but we will be under the influence of the Spirit (where God will do the work for us).

So we see that when God is in control of our lives, the soul is in complete submission to the Spirit, and we can accomplish things that we cannot accomplish when the flesh is in control. As a result of this truth, Paul tells us of the actions or reactions that we might find in one who is under the leading of the soul. Now, understand that when someone walks after the flesh, their fruit, or outcome, may appear good or bad. There is good flesh and there is bad flesh. We will discuss the good flesh during our later discussion of the fruit of the Spirit. For now, let's look at the bad flesh that is discussed in verses 19-21.

Now the works of the flesh are manifest, which are these; adultery, fornication, uncleanness, lasciviousness, idolatry, witchcraft, hatred, variance, emulations, wrath, strife, seditions, heresies, envyings, murders, drunkenness, revellings, and such like.

The phrase *works of the flesh* means "the efforts of the soul under the influence of the body." *Manifest* means "to make evident." Therefore, when the body is in control of our soul, it is often evident by our behavior. Let us define some of this behavior.

Adultery: Sex outside of marriage
Fornication: Sex before marriage
Uncleanness: Sexual deviance
Lasciviousness: Sexual excess

These behaviors describe fleshly acts that are sexual immorality. Now consider this fact, lest we believe we are too moral to behave in such wicked ways, Paul then lists some other lusts of the flesh that may at times seem attractive to the soul:

Idolatry: Valuing something more than you value your relationship with God
Witchcraft: Sorcery; being under the influence of demonic forces
Hatred: Having a great dislike for another
Variance: Argumentative
Emulation: An unhealthy desire for superiority
Wrath: Revengeful feelings of getting even
Strife: Spreading angry contention
Sedition: Raising commotion
Heresies: Errors in the fundamentals of religion
Envying: A general uneasiness with the happiness of others

Murder: The premeditated killing of another human

Drunkenness: To be habitually overpowered with intoxication from alcohol

Reveling: Uncontrolled feasting and carousing in a party-like atmosphere

Now, I see that some of these things have been and are at times problems for me. And when they are, it is made evident that I am exercising the lusts of my flesh. I am obviously following after the flesh, because I am doing bad things of the flesh. If this is a consistent problem in your life and there is no conviction or chastening from God, then you should question your salvation. That's what I believe Paul means when he says, *of the which I tell you before, as I have also told you in time past, that they which do such things shall not inherit the kingdom of God.*

It is usually obvious when someone is engaged in these sins. Many, if not all, of them, are noticeable by outward demonstrations of behavior. That is why Paul said that these works of the flesh are manifest, or made evident. It's bad flesh. The fruit of the Spirit contrasts it. However, I want to tell you about another type of flesh. It is a flesh that hardly anyone knows anything about. Paul alluded to it in Galatians 3:1 as a type of flesh that bewitches, or fascinates, Christians. It is not a flesh that is evident by our behavior. As a matter of fact, it is very hard to discern. It is less evident. It is the biggest problem, in my opinion, in Christianity today. I call it "doing good in the flesh." Galatians 5:19-21 lists bad flesh [unrighteousness] and verses 22-23 list righteous behavior. This "good" flesh is neither *unrighteous* behavior, nor *righteous* behavior. So what was Paul referring to? It's *self-righteous* behavior.

You see, the devil knows that believers are not going to be comfortable with the Holy Spirit convicting them of engaging in the works of the flesh mentioned in verses 19-21. God's people may vary from the Spirit's leading and walk after the flesh, but being in Christ, this type of behavior brings great conviction as well as chastening from the Lord.

So, the devil has created a more subtle type of flesh that hardly anybody realizes. The Bible says that Satan is transformed into an angel of light (2 Corinthians 11:14). He can appear as a provider of spiritual direction. He uses this imposter-like spiritual direction to lead us into doing good in our own power rather than in the power of God. That is good flesh. Doing good under the influence of the soul instead of under the power of the Spirit is a fascinating place to be – yet it still falls under the category of trying to use a fleshly weapon to fight a fleshly temptation.

Let's return to the discussion of lusts of the flesh as outlined in Galatians 5. This is the second time the church in Galatia has been explained this truth. We don't know exactly the circumstances in which it was previously used. Maybe it was in an unmentioned sermon that Paul preached to this church (he had been there once prior to this letter), or possibly that the churches would share their letters that Paul wrote to them. If that were the case, then he could be discussing the nearly identical passage that he wrote to the church in Corinth in which he said:

> *Know ye not that the unrighteous shall not inherit the kingdom of God? Be not deceived: neither fornicators, nor idolaters, nor adulterers, nor effeminate, nor abusers of themselves with mankind, Nor thieves, nor covetous, nor drunkards, nor revilers, nor extortioners, shall inherit the kingdom of God* (1 Corinthians 6:9-10).

These fleshly behaviors are qualities of one who is not submitting to the inner man, God is not in control of their lives, and the soul is not in complete submission to the Spirit. There is, however, an alternative. I call it "a little heaven on earth." That alternative is the victorious Christian life! This means that God lives through us, giving us an opportunity to live a heaven-like lifestyle here while guaranteeing us a future in heaven.

Unfortunately, all of us have been guilty of one or more of these sins at one time or another. But verse 11 gives us hope: *And such were some of you: but ye are washed, but ye are sanctified, but ye are justified in the name of the Lord Jesus, and by the Spirit of our God.*

Wow! What a marvelous opportunity! God has offered to clean house. Mine and yours. He can wash us from the filthiness of our sins through justification and sanctification. We are justified by belief in the Lord Jesus and sanctified through the influence of the Spirit of God – not by our own works and certainly not by the flesh.

Remember, as we face fleshly temptations we must use the weapons *God* offers. Fighting the flesh with the flesh just doesn't work!

We Lose Our Freedom to Choose When We Give In to Temptation and Its Consequences. Instead, Make Fruitful Choices for Positive Consequences.

Let the wicked forsake his way, and the unrighteous man his thoughts: and let him return unto the LORD and he will have mercy upon him; and to our God, for he will abundantly pardon. —Isaiah 55:7

When we first take hold of a vice, it is extremely pleasurable. It may even seem to be the only time we feel happy, the only time we experience any comfort in our lives. However, the Bible warns in Proverbs 20:17, *Bread of deceit is sweet to a man; but afterwards his mouth shall be filled with gravel.* You can clearly see that while deceitful and wrong actions may bring temporary pleasure, afterwards it leaves a very bad taste in your mouth. The consequences for your behavior then belong to God. Proverbs 9:17-18 indicates that, *Stolen waters are sweet, and bread eaten in secret is pleasant. But he knoweth not that the dead are there; and that her guests are in the depths of hell.* No matter how much enjoyment we may receive from our stubborn habit or addiction, we can be sure that the consequences are never worth it.

We must realize that God is watching us. He watches every single thing we do. Proverbs 5:21 says, *For the ways of man are before the eyes of the LORD, and he pondereth all his goings.* That word *ponders* means to "weigh, or consider." What does He consider? He considers the proper actions that should be taken against our behavior to bring a proper reaction from us. His desire is for a repentance and a dependence on Him, rather than on some vice that only brings temporal advice. Look at the warning that is given in the very next verse and ask yourself if you are in this position. *His own iniquities shall take the wicked himself, and he shall be holden with the cords of his sins* (Proverbs 5:22). This verse clearly indicates that once we grab hold of a wicked vice, that it will begin to wrap itself around us. Though at the beginning we may be able to get out of its hold, eventually the cord will be tightened around us and we will be held in bondage with the cords of our sin. Oh, how that is what happened to me!

Next is the important warning to those of us who struggle to fight back: *He shall die without instruction; and in the greatness of his folly he shall go astray* (Proverbs 5:23). This consequence (going astray, which leads to a premature physical and spiritual death) cannot be monitored by us. It is determined by God. Until that unfortunate time that we experience this untimely demise, we will live among consequences that are designed to bring us back to God. The cure is found in Isaiah 55:7: *Let the wicked forsake his way* [#1], *and the unrighteous man his thoughts* [#2], *and let him return unto the LORD* [#3] *and he will have mercy upon him; and to our God, for he will abundantly pardon.* We need God's mercy [not getting what we deserve]. We need God's pardon [penalty removed for what we've done] so that we may start over. That is accomplished by simply turning from our way of doing things and from our way of thinking and returning to the Lord.

The key is to learn how to choose God's way in the first place.

Choosing God's Way: The Fear of the Lord

The fear of the Lord is an awe or respect of who God is and what He can do. It is respect for what God could do, what God would do, and what God should do. God alone is in control of what He does *to* us and what He does *for* us. When we walk with the Lord, He may do many things for us. He can increase our health, our wealth, our joy, our anointing, our livelihood, our productivity, our lifespan, and many, many other blessings to those whose hearts are stayed on Him. This ability of our God to bless our obedience should be of great importance to us. It should lead us to an awe and respect of *who* God is and *what* He is willing to do. To be able to do all of these few things I've listed is an impossibility for anyone other than God. That is how powerful He is.

Of course, when we walk in disobedience to God, He is equally capable and just to punish our wrong behavior, as well. As noted in this chapter's principle, the consequences are inevitable, incalculable, and up to God. When we are wrong, God has options to use for our benefit and to increase our fear of Him. He has the option of judgment. This is getting what we deserve, usually in the form of chastening. It is intended to bring about repentance.

With repentance should come an increase in our fear of the Lord. He also has the option of mercy. *Mercy* is not getting what we deserve. God has often chosen to use mercy on His people for their benefit and to increase our fear of Him. Finally, He has the option for grace. *Grace* is getting what you do not deserve-God's unmerited favor. Grace, without question, will always create a personal benefit and should increase our fear of the Lord.

I believe God's favorite way of increasing our fear of Him when we are engaged in wrongdoing is by granting mercy: not giving the wrongdoer what they deserved for doing wrong. This is so obvious in Scripture. The word *mercy* appears over three hundred times in the Bible, and nearly every time, it is referring to the mercy of God toward a wrongdoer.

In Psalm 147:11, we see that *the LORD taketh pleasure in them that fear him, in those that hope in his mercy.* It pleases God when we fear Him, and this fear makes itself evident in a hope for mercy. *Hope* means "an expectation of obtaining a desire. In this case, the desire that we expect to obtain is mercy. Dissected and defined, the Lord is teaching us that our fear is proven with an expectation that God is capable of not giving us what we deserve. Now, of course, receiving that mercy is not dependent on our expectation but on God's goodness toward us. However, God is pleased when we realize our need and place our hope for mercy in Him.

God wants us to realize He is the Source of every good thing. When something goes right, respect God for what He has done. When something goes wrong, respect God for what He is doing (Romans 8:28). If you will do this, it will change the influence that sin has on your life. God's formula for removing us from evil behavior and influence is found in Proverbs 16:6, *By mercy and truth iniquity is purged: and by the fear of the LORD men depart from evil.* By God *not* giving us what we deserve and our willingness as a result of that mercy to conform to what is right, we will purge iniquity from our lives. This mercy should increase our fear of the Lord. If it does, then we will depart from evil. If His mercy does not increase our fear of the Lord, then we will not depart from evil and God will replace His mercy, in His time, with judgment!

Hope for His mercy. Conform to what is right and let the experience produce a respect and awe for our all-powerful God. You will depart from evil and bring great pleasure to God.

Choosing God's Way: After the Spirit, In the Spirit

Let's look at a few verses in Romans 8 to better understand the difference between being "in the flesh" and walking "after the flesh." Understanding these terms will help us better understand what it means to walk "in the Spirit" and "after the Spirit."

This is not a complete study, but rather a short explanation of these two terms. Do not skim the verses. That will hinder your study. Read each verse slowly, meditate on the meaning, and notice especially the emphasis added where underlined.

> **Romans 8:1:** *There is therefore now no condemnation to them which are* in *Christ Jesus, who walk not after the flesh, but after the Spirit.*
>
> **Romans 8:2:** *For the law of the Spirit of life in Christ Jesus hath made me free from the law of sin and death.*
>
> **Romans 8:3:** *For what the law could not do, in that it was weak through the flesh, God sending his own Son in the likeness of sinful flesh, and for sin, condemned sin in the flesh:* (Reread verse one, then continue to verse four.)
>
> **Romans 8:4:** *That the righteousness of the law might be fulfilled in us, who walk not after the flesh, but after the Spirit.*
>
> **Romans 8:5:** *For they that are after the flesh do mind the things of the flesh; but they that are after the Spirit the things of the Spirit.*
>
> **Romans 8:8:** *So then they that are in the flesh* [those who are unsaved] *cannot please God.*

Romans 8:9: *But ye are not in the flesh, but in the Spirit, if so be that the Spirit of God dwell in you.*

Romans 8:10: *And if Christ be in you, the body is dead because of sin; but the Spirit is life because of righteousness.*

Verse 1 tells us that if we are in Christ, we will not be condemned. It goes on to indicate that if we walk after the flesh and not after the Spirit, we could experience condemnation. And we do! Not from God, but from the devil. That is how we can explain such horrible feelings of condemnation when we behave badly. That does not come from God, it comes from the devil. But if we are walking after the Spirit, those feelings of condemnation will be an impossibility. There is a big difference between the Spirit's conviction and Satan's condemnation.

This new law (verse two) of the Spirit brings us emancipation from the power of sin and freedom from God's condemnation. The word *law* means "rule of conduct." He is telling us that if we will yield to the rule of conduct that now lives within us, we will experience the benefits of being free from the power of sin. We have chosen freedom. If we don't yield to the Spirit's rule for conducting ourselves, we will instead walk "after the flesh." We are free from sin's power, but as a result of our walk, we will not exercise or experience the benefits of this freedom. We are willfully walking after the flesh, following it as it is leading us astray, and lose our freedom to choose by not exercising our freedom after the Spirit.

This is often a result of the presence of fear or a weakness in our faith. Either we fear failing in our new-found freedom so we choose to remain in unbound bondage, or we lack faith that God is really going to do what He said He will do.

I have heard it said that after the Emancipation Proclamation was signed, a large number of former slaves became afraid of the ramifications of their new freedom, and they determined to remain slaves. Free as they were, they chose to remain in bondage and under tribute to their masters. This choice did not change the fact that they were free, but they remained as they had been.

That is exactly what we are capable of doing after conversion. Though God has freed us from the power of sin, we can still choose to follow it. It has no power over us except what we give it. To stop following after this illegitimate master, all we have to do is exercise our faith in the law that liberated us. For the law of the Spirit of life in Christ Jesus has made us free from the law of sin and death!

Verse 3 reminds us that those that are "in the flesh" are condemned. Verse 4 proves that we can live the Christian life by yielding to the inner man and not going after what is already dead (verse 10). Verse 8 tells us that those in the flesh cannot please God; to please God we must walk in the Spirit by faith. Verse 9 reminds us of our position in Christ and His position in us.

Are we in the flesh or in the Spirit? Are we walking after the flesh or after the Spirit? These are fundamental choices that will determine the degree to which we experience freedom in Jesus Christ, and exhibit the fruit of the Spirit.

Choosing God's Way: The Fruit of the Spirit

Let us now look at the fruit of the Spirit as listed in Galatians 5:22-23: *But the fruit of the Spirit is love, joy, peace, longsuffering, gentleness, goodness, faith, meekness, temperance...*

Fruit means "outcome or result." Thus, the *fruit of the Spirit* means "the outcome, or result, of the Spirit's leading in our lives." By design, God has limited Himself in the way in which He will respond to all forms of adversity. This was His decision. The Spirit will lead you to respond in one of these nine ways, or He will not lead you to respond to a circumstance whatsoever. It is His choice how to respond, and it is our choice to yield to that response.

Realizing that God has nine actions or reactions to all the circumstances in life and the devil is an angel of light that mimics false spiritual direction thereby offering an alternative to each of these fruits, then how many potential actions or reactions do we have to choose from? Of course that would be eighteen. It is actually twenty when you consider that God may ask you to not respond and the devil leads you to respond anyway, or He may ask you to respond and you decide not to. So there are basically twenty options for every circumstance in life. I know that makes life problems sound simplistic, but that is an aberration. The majority of the flaw in Christian evangelism of the lost can be traced to Christians' inability to develop a dynamic enough walk with God to determine the difference between *righteous* responses under the influence of the Spirit and *self-righteous* responses under the influence of the flesh.

Let's look at these eighteen potential actions or reactions of a Spirit led or self led Christian to all the circumstances in life. We will look at them in breakdowns of three and as listed in order in the Bible. They will be categorized using the following descriptions:

- **Transforming**—Love, Joy and Peace. That is inner being transformation.
- **Conforming**—Longsuffering, Gentleness, and Goodness. That is outer being conformation.
- **Reforming**—Faith, Meekness and Temperance. That is new being reformation.

I call the first breakdown and first three fruits of the Spirit "inner being transformation." A person will never change the way they act until they change the way they think. God must change the inside of the man first and foremost.

If you will notice, the first three fruits of the Spirit as listed in the Bible are all fruits that deal with the inside behaviors of a man. If a man does not love, or have joy or peace, it can go undetected. It is an inside problem. Before you can get a man to act right on the outside, you should get him to act right on the inside. God wants our inner being to act right. He offers these three fruits to be our inner man's response to adversity. If our soul will yield to our inner man than we will respond properly. Let's take a look at God's three internal responses found within our inner man.

Transforming: The Choice Between Love and Self-Love

There are different types of love mentioned in the Bible. Unlike in the English language, there are several Greek words for love. *Eros,* from which we get the word *erotic,* means "physical love." In Greek mythology, Eros was the god of love, which we would associate with the Roman god Cupid. The word *eros* is not used anywhere in the New Testament. *Philadelphia* means "brotherly love." It is derived from the root word *philos,* which means "affectionate regard; fondness." It is the type of love shared between close friends. *Philostorgos* means "family affection," and is translated as "kindly affection" in the New Testament. It is the type of love we have for our parents or our children.

There is another Greek word for love in its highest form: *agape.* It is the word Paul used when he listed the fruit of the Spirit, "love." The best definition of *agape* is "the willing, sacrificial giving of oneself for the benefit of others without thought of return." That is God's kind of love, and it is available for us to demonstrate to others by the power of the Holy Spirit.

This type of love is evident in many places in Scripture, but never was more love shown to us than by our Creator, the God of heaven. In John 3:16 we read, *For God so loved the world, that he gave his only begotten Son, that whosoever believeth in him should not perish, but have everlasting life.* What did God do to demonstrate His love toward us? He willingly, sacrificially gave of Himself for the benefit of others without thought of return. That is the greatest gift of all! He did not even require us to change before He would offer this gift to us. In Romans 5:8 we read, *But God commendeth his love toward us, in that, while we were yet sinners, Christ died for us.*

Yet God was not alone in this demonstration of love. His only begotten Son was a willing sacrifice for God's plan to redeem sinful man. Though Christ desired for another way instead of His own death, He was willing to lay down His life for us. Christ, under the influence of the Spirit, yielded to love, the fruit of the Spirit, and gave Himself for us. In Ephesians 5:2, Paul encourages us to walk in love like Christ walked in love. He is indicating a "following after." Christ followed the Spirit's leading and expressed God's love toward us. We ought also to follow Christ's example and follow the Spirit's leading to express God's love toward others. As Paul worded it, *And walk in love, as Christ also hath loved us, and hath given himself for us an offering and a sacrifice to God for a sweet smelling savour* (Ephesians 5:2).

As a matter of fact, if we do not yield to God's leading to demonstrate love toward others, they will not be convinced that we are believers in and followers of Christ. This is taught, by Jesus himself in John 13:34-35: *A new commandment I give unto you, That ye love one another; as I have loved you, that ye also love one another. By this shall all men know that ye are my disciples, if ye have love one to another.*

We are commanded throughout the Word of God to love others and one another. God the Father set the perfect example. Christ, in the power of the Holy Spirit, yielded to that example, and we ought to, also. It is a command for us to love. And, the truth is, all true love comes from God; it is simply yielded to by man.

First John 3:23 says, *And this is his commandment, That we should believe on the name of his Son Jesus Christ, and love one another, as he gave us commandment.* And Matthew 22:37-40 records that Jesus taught,

> *Thou shalt love the Lord thy God with all thy heart, and with all thy soul, and with all thy mind. This is the first and great commandment. And the second is like unto it, Thou shalt love thy neighbour as thyself. On these two commandments hang all the law and the prophets.*

He is asking us to willingly and sacrificially give of ourselves for the benefit of God and others. Love is God's tool for showing unselfish favor to undeserving people.

We can do many things for undeserving people. We can make many sacrifices. Yet if those acts of kindness are not done under the influence of the Spirit's love, we will not bring a positive effect into that person's life, no matter what our level of sacrifice. Let's take a look at 1 Corinthians 13:1-3 to see what God says about sacrifices that do not demonstrate His love:

> *Though I speak with the tongues of men and of angels, and have not charity, I am become as sounding brass, or a tinkling cymbal. And though I have the gift of prophecy, and understand all mysteries, and all knowledge; and though I have all faith, so that I could remove mountains, and have not charity, I am nothing. And though I bestow all my goods to feed the poor, and though I give my body to be burned, and have not charity, it profiteth me nothing.*

Fleshly Sacrifice: Eloquent speaking of various languages
End Result Without Love: They are of no more value to the hearer than notes of a trumpet or the crash of a cymbal.

Fleshly Sacrifice: Great understanding of God and His ways as well as an ability to communicate those truths and to live them as well
End Result Without Love: You amount to nothing in their eyes. They will not be impressed with our apparent spiritual gifts.

Fleshly Sacrifice: Give all my possessions to feed the weak and needy and sacrifice my life for the same
End Result Without Love: These great sacrifices will be of no profit to the giver in this life nor in the next life.

However, we then read in verses 4-8 of the great value our works will have if we add to these sacrifices a yielding to love, the fruit of the Spirit. Let's take a look at this:

> *Charity suffereth long, and is kind; charity envieth not; charity vaunteth not itself, is not puffed up, Doth not behave itself unseemly, seeketh not her own, is not easily provoked, thinketh no evil; Rejoiceth not in iniquity, but rejoiceth in the truth; Beareth all things, believeth all things, hopeth all things, endureth all things. Charity never faileth:*

Suffereth long, and is kind: Puts up with inconveniences
Envieth not: Lifts up others, not self
Vaunteth not itself: Is not stuck up
Doth not behave itself unseemly: Acts in right and godly ways
Seeketh not her own: Looks for what is right
Is not easily provoked: Responds in right and godly ways
Thinketh no evil: Thinks right and godly thoughts
Rejoiceth not in iniquity: Doesn't get excited about what is not right
Rejoiceth in the truth: Gets excited about what is right
Beareth all things: Carries the weight OF WHAT?
Believeth all things: Gives the benefit of the doubt
Hopeth all things: Hopes for the best
Endureth all things: Keeps on keeping on
Never fails: Works every time!

Honestly, does our service for God and others manifest itself in the proper behaviors listed above? Sometimes, yes; but other times, no. It's as if our love is genuine and our hearts are pure, yet we tend to behave in a somewhat selfish manner when we are expressing love. Why is this? It is simple to explain but not so readily recognized in our lives. The opportunity to yield to the fruit of the Spirit, love, has a fleshly alternative. This fleshly alternative to God's love flowing through us is not something that will appear to be the opposite of love. We would not easily fall for the devil's influence to yield to doing the work of the flesh—hate! The devil knows this, so he stimulates a flesh that is so often misunderstood by both the doer and the receiver of the good deeds. Once again, it's the flesh of self-righteousness. The devil's option for us is to show love in our own power. It is not God's love. It is our love. It is otherwise known as self-love.

Our expressions of the fruit of the Spirit~Love, when understood by the recipient, will rarely be rejected. When love is misunderstood or rejected it is because there are so many false manifestations of it. Remember, love is the willing, sacrificial giving of oneself for the benefit of others without thought of return. However, the fleshly alternative of self-love is the willing or unwilling giving of oneself to benefit others with selfish thoughts of return.

The true test of a servant is if he acts like one when he is being treated like one.

I once had a student who had slipped in his recovery and engaged in drug use. He appeared genuinely repentant for what he had done. I asked him to explain the events that led up to his relapse. He said it was because he did not believe that his wife loved him. Well, I found that hard to believe. While he was away on his binge, his wife had demonstrated her love for him in many ways.

I asked him, "What makes you think that your wife does not love you?" He replied, "Because I work hard all week long at my job and provide a good living for my family. All I ask for is a hot meal and some clean clothes. I come home tired at night and have to eat something she just threw together or picked up at a drive through. She never does laundry until after it piles up, and the house is always a mess!"

Now I knew something he had failed to mention. His wife worked full-time as a nurse, twelve-hour shifts and often up to 60 hours per week. Of course, his forty-hour-a-week office job did not afford him time to mow the lawn or take out the trash, so he paid a neighbor boy (out of his wife's wages) to do his exterior work. And, she also cared for her three children that were all under the age of eight. I wouldn't know, but I am told that men can surely be pigs!

Now, ladies, stop showing this last paragraph to your husband; I am not talking about him! But, suffice it to say, both parties in that marriage seriously misunderstood each other's problems. She believed that his biggest problem was that he had a drug addiction, and he believed that his wife did not love him. Both conclusions were wrong. The primary problem was that the husband did not love his wife – that is, not the way God wants him to love her. You see, he was somewhat willingly (yet begrudgingly) and sacrificially giving for the benefit of his wife, but he had selfish thoughts of return. (His wife probably did, too.) He gave to his wife, but he wanted her to give back. And that seems fair, but self-love, when given, demands a return. By contrast, God's love demands nothing in return.

Jesus was not merely making a suggestion when He said, *This is my commandment, That ye love one another, as I have loved you. Greater love hath no man than this, that a man lay down his life for his friends* (John 15:12-13). He was asking us to choose the transforming power of the fruit of the Spirit called "love."

Transforming: The Choice Between Joy and Frustration

Joy is, of course, one of the most enjoyable fruits of the Spirit to experience, but also one of the most difficult fruits to yield to. It is strange to realize and difficult to understand that when we lack joy, it is only because we have failed to yield to it. *Joy* is "a cheerful, calm delight in all the circumstances of life."

God will place each of us in situations that will try our faith, produce some patience, and generate a joy found only in the Holy Spirit. We will only grow and develop when the outer man is wounded by circumstances in life and we are given opportunities to yield to the inner man. As a result, we will become less carnal and more Spirit-led. The more Spirit-led we are, the more like Christ we are and the more power we experience. Living a Christ-like life under the power of the Holy Spirit is the best way to influence others for Christ, maximizing our God-given gifts for the benefit of family, the church, and the kingdom. It is the life of Christ flowing through us.

We see this truth taught in Romans 8:28-29:

> *And we know that all things work together for good to them that love God, to them who are the called according to his purpose. For whom he did foreknow, he also did predestinate to be conformed to the image of his Son, that he might be the firstborn among many brethren.*

All things: Everything, good and bad
Work together: Produce a result
For good: In a way that is advantageous
Love God: Willingly give of oneself without thought of return
Called… to his purpose: to be conformed to the image of His Son
Foreknow: Know in advance
Predestinate: Plan or ordain in advance
Conformed: Poured into the mold
Image of his Son: The likeness of Christ
Firstborn: The first in order of birth
Among many brethren: People who become believers after and as a result of new birth through faith in Christ Jesus

This passage sheds light on the whole subject of Christians experiencing adversity, trials, and persecution. It tells us that everything that happens to us, both good and bad, is intended to produce an advantageous result. But we must give of ourselves for God's benefit and allow ourselves to be molded into the likeness of Christ. God knew in advance that He would effect this type of development in our lives. This method is designed by God to draw others to Christ because of our example.

I have explained all of this to help you understand the danger of rejecting the Spirit's gift of joy. You see, when a difficult circumstance arises, we are actually being blessed with the opportunity to experience joy. We can rejoice and calmly delight in that circumstance. A moment of meditation will serve to remind us that it is for our good and God's glory. It will further serve to remind us that by rejoicing in that circumstance, we could be leading another person closer to becoming a fellow brother or sister in Christ.

Responding with joy in a particular circumstance will likely result in the wounding of the outer man and the shining forth of the inner man. Often, we will see circumstances fade away or become easier to manage when we allow all things to work together for good, properly responding to adversity. However, the devil has an alternative to all of this, a different way to face difficult circumstances: regret. Satan's option is to respond to bad circumstances in our own power. It does not produce God's joy; it produces our own level of contentment. It is otherwise known as frustration, which is "a rejection or unhappy refusal in the cicumstances of life."

When we face an unwanted circumstance, we can either respond with joy or frustration. The truth is that most of our brothers and sisters in Christ will accept either response. Others will either appreciate and respect us for our willingness to respond to joy when faced with adversity, or they will pity us as we respond to the circumstances with feelings of frustration. It is sad but true that most Christians do not see frustration as a work of the flesh. However, it is a response generated by the soul. It stems from a negative thought, desire, or emotion. When the heart responds to adversity by looking to the soul for a response, we are *guaranteed* to act after the flesh.

It has been said by many when counseling, "I understand your frustration." That's like saying, "I understand your crack cocaine addiction." Good flesh is as bad as bad flesh. Flesh is flesh, and we cannot please God if we are walking after the flesh, no matter how much good we are doing, no matter how much we believe our frustration is justified.

To this end, we must understand God's purposes for adversity:

- To wound the outer man
- To allow the inner man to shine through
- To display our love for God
- To conform us to be like Christ
- To lead others to salvation in Christ

If we respond after the flesh in a difficult circumstance, then we will be forced to continue facing this circumstance over and over again to bring about God's determined results. Furthermore, if we will not yield to joy, we may suffer more severe circumstances. God is faithful to break down our flesh and develop His Spirit. If you want to be like Christ, you can be! But you must allow God to place you into circumstances that will wound you. Then, you must respond properly to that circumstance. When you do, you will come forth a vessel for the finer (Proverbs 25:4).

Even if you did not understand these truths before reading them, you can probably look back and see that this has been the routine of your life. Accept it and it gets better, or reject it and it gets worse. Though you may have never known the reason why it was that way, now you do. Praise the Lord! Yielding to joy brings Christ-likeness and the conversion of unbelievers.

You have a choice: the fruit of the Spirit, joy, or the work of the flesh: frustration. It is not a work of the flesh that is obvious. It is often hard to discern. But a refusal to rejoice in the circumstances of life is, indeed, the lust of the flesh we call "frustration."

Transforming: The Choice Between Peace and Worry

Peace is a most necessary fruit to which we must yield when facing adversity and persecution in the Christian life. *Peace* is "to be safe from harm in spirit, mind, and body." Why is this such a necessary fruit? Christians who yield to the fruit of love and joy are under the influence of God. They live godly lives because they are "in Christ." And what does the Bible say about Christians who live godly lives in Christ Jesus? I think you know, but let's look at 2 Timothy 3:10-12:

> But thou hast fully known my doctrine, manner
> of life, purpose, faith, longsuffering, charity, patience,
> Persecutions, afflictions, which came unto me at Anti-
> och, at Iconium, at Lystra; Yea, and all that will live
> godly in Christ Jesus shall suffer persecution.

Paul explained to Timothy that if he lived a godly life under the influence of the Spirit, then he could expect to suffer persecution. Persecution in the twenty-first century is one of the most misunderstood of Christian experiences. If we were to ask most godly believers if they suffered persecution, they would say no. They think of persecution as maybe being stoned to death or maybe martyred in some other way for the cause of the Gospel. And while it can include those types of horrible experiences, the basic definition of *persecution* is "a pursuit, for the purpose of oppression."

Paul's godly living led him to be persecuted in three places: Antioch, Iconium, and Lystra. Let's look at what Paul referred to as "persecution" during his trips to these three cities, beginning with Antioch:

> And the next sabbath day came almost the whole
> city together to hear the word of God. But when the
> Jews saw the multitudes, they were filled with envy, and
> spake against those things which were spoken by Paul,
> contradicting and blaspheming (Acts 13:44-45).

Here we see Paul being contradicted and blasphemed by the Jewish religious leaders because they were jealous. Why were they jealous? Because almost the whole city came out to hear Paul preaching the Word of God. He was effective at reaching a crowd because he did it the right way. As a result, He and Barnabas experienced criticism and disagreements by the Jewish people who were lovers of God but non-believers in Jesus. And in 2 Timothy 3, Paul called this type of behavior persecution!

But where were the stones? Where were the physical assaults? They threw nothing but verbal attacks. Paul said that because of living godly in Christ, they were persecuted. He considered this verbal abuse to be persecution. They could have responded by quitting the ministry. They could have at least ceased to submit to the Spirit's leading and brought an end to their verbal persecution, but they did not.

Instead, Paul responded to peace. The next verse says that they "waxed bold." This means they grew in courage in the face of persecution. God was in control, Paul knew that he was safe from harm in his spirit, mind, and body. The word *spirit* here in our definition is speaking of temperament. It is the seat of passions. Paul didn't get overly excited that he might be in harm's way. He didn't begin to fret in his mind or fear for the protection of his body. He responded by continuing to minister, but, as God must have led, to a different strain of people – the Gentiles. *Then Paul and Barnabas waxed bold, and said, It was necessary that the word of God should first have been spoken to you: but seeing ye put it from you, and judge yourselves unworthy of everlasting life, lo, we turn to the Gentiles* (Acts 13:46).

Paul could have selfishly focused on his own benefit and responded with frustration, missing God's plan for his life. Instead, Paul and Barnabas continued in the peace of God.

They would meet persecution again in Iconium:

> *And it came to pass in Iconium, that they went both together into the synagogue of the Jews, and so spake, that a great multitude both of the Jews and also of the Greeks believed. But the unbelieving Jews stirred up the Gentiles, and made their minds evil*

affected against the brethren. Long time therefore abode they speaking boldly in the Lord, which gave testimony unto the word of his grace, and granted signs and wonders to be done by their hands. But the multitude of the city was divided: and part held with the Jews, and part with the apostles. And when there was an assault made both of the Gentiles, and also of the Jews with their rulers, to use them despitefully, and to stone them, They were ware of it, and fled unto Lystra and Derbe, cities of Lycaonia, and unto the region that lieth round about: And there they preached the gospel (Acts 14:1-7).

Paul and Barnabas had been extremely effective. Many Jews (on whom Paul was less focused as a result of his trip to Antioch) and Greeks [Gentiles] believed their message. Lo and behold, here comes the persecution! But not with flying rocks or even verbal assaults. No, this time it was the unbelieving Jews inciting the Gentiles. (Notice they did not try to persuade the multitude of believing Jews—it was too late; they had already believed!) They instigated a tumult among the people by poisoning their minds with criticism against Paul and Barnabas. Yet another "pursuit of oppression" against these Spirit-led believers!

Their response was the same as before, but in a different direction this time. Verse 3 says, *Long time therefore abode they speaking boldly in the Lord.* The word *therefore* brings two statements together. Because of their effectiveness, they decided not only to stay in Iconium, but to also continue speaking—boldly! They relied on the fruit of the Spirit, peace, to help them face persecution while they continued preaching. Consequently, God's power became even more evident as He granted these godly men the ability to perform signs and wonders.

But things only seemed to get worse. The people became divided: the believers versus the unbelievers. In verses 4 and 5, we see this division reaching the boiling point. *But the multitude of the city was divided: and part held with the Jews, and part with the apostles. And... there was an assault made both of the Gentiles, and also of the Jews with their rulers, to use them despitefully, and to stone them.*

To use them despitefully means "a reproach that attempts physical injury." This conflict had grown from openly verbal contradiction in Antioch to verbal criticism behind their backs and led up to a desire for physical injury. This mob wanted to stone them for what the Jewish leaders considered blasphemy.

Paul responded in the same way that Jesus did when He was faced with popular uprisings: He and Barnabas left Iconium and they did so in a hurry. They yielded to peace by retreating, thus rejecting its alternative. Had they stayed, there would have been a riot of sorts between the believers and the unbelievers.

What was God's higher purpose for this persecution? We find one answer in Acts 16:1. *Then came he to Derbe and Lystra: and, behold, a certain disciple was there, named Timotheus, the son of a certain woman, which was a Jewess, and believed; but his father was a Greek.* As a result of their stalled work in Iconium and the resulting physical pursuit of oppression, they went to these cities in Lycaonia and met young Timothy. What a blessing and benefit Timothy became to these persecuted believers! Yet, the persecution followed them, and this time it actually led to physical injury. Let's take a look at Acts 14:19-21 and the events in Lystra:

> *And there came thither certain Jews from Antioch and Iconium, who persuaded the people, and, having stoned Paul, drew him out of the city, supposing he had been dead. Howbeit, as the disciples stood round about him, he rose up, and came into the city: and the next day he departed with Barnabas to Derbe. And...they... preached the gospel to that city; and had taught many.*

The same troublemakers from Antioch and Iconium caught up with Paul, but did he fear? No, not at all. Stoned and left for dead by these attackers, he revived and returned to the city to preach the gospel. What an unbelievable measure of peace God gave Paul! He was so free from worry of harm to his spirit, mind, and body that he had no fear of man. He and Barnabas then *returned again to Lystra, and to Iconium, and Antioch, Confirming the souls of the disciples, and exhorting them to continue in the faith, and that we must through much tribulation enter into the kingdom of God* (verses 21-22).

Unbelievable! They returned straight into the fire! They went right back to the same places where they had come under great verbal and physical persecution, encouraging fellow Christians to continue in their bold belief of God's system of management [faith]. Seeing these truths helps me understand better what Paul was saying when he wrote to the church of Phillipi, *And the peace of God, which passeth all understanding, shall keep your hearts and minds through Christ Jesus* (Philippians 4:7).

How does Paul's lesson on peace in the face of persecution conclude? Let's look at 2 Timothy 3:11-14:

> *Persecutions, afflictions, which came unto me at Antioch, at Iconium, at Lystra; what persecutions I endured: but out of them all the Lord delivered me. Yea, and all that will live godly in Christ Jesus shall suffer persecution. But evil men and seducers shall wax worse and worse, deceiving, and being deceived. But continue thou in the things which thou hast learned and hast been assured of, knowing of whom thou hast learned them.*

Paul opens our eyes about living godly under the influence of Christ. As a Christian, you will suffer pursuits of oppression from people you try to help. It may be verbal to your face and/or behind your back. If you respond properly, God's power will be on your life.

You may also be attacked physically, but do not worry and do not retaliate. Plunge into God's perfect peace and boldly continue to do what God leads you to do, and you will be delivered.

Below, I have included part of a song that so eloquently reminds us of the truth of God's ability to protect us in times of persecution and adversity.

God on the Mountain

(Tracy Darrt)
Life is easy when you're up on the mountain
And you've got peace of mind like you've never known.
But then things change and you're down in the valley.
Don't lose faith for you're never alone.

For the God on the mountain is still God in the valley.
When things go wrong, He'll make it right.
And the God of the good times is still God in the bad times.
The God of the day is still God in the night.

Remember, there is nothing more attractive to a lost person than someone who loves unconditionally, expresses great joy in life's adversities, and exhibits a peace that surpasses understanding in the face of opposition. At the same time, there is nothing more hypocritical to a lost person than self-centered, frustrated people that call themselves Christians.

Once again, for every fruit that God offers, there is a fleshly alternative. The alternative to the peace, the fruit of the Spirit, is worry. Worry is "to live in fear of harm in your spirit, mind, AND body." This alternative to the fruit of peace is a poor testimony to those who are observing our walk with the Lord.

I have met a lot of Christians who live much of their lives worrying about things. I am guilty, at times, of yielding to my soul's fear of harm, as well. I believe the reason we struggle with fear is because our godly living is sometimes done under an influence other than the influence of Christ.

The most realistic way to differentiate between peace and worry is found in the eye of the beholder. God is the true judge of what is harmful for us. He will not harm us. Everything is going to work together for our good. As a result, the persecutions of life will never bring us harm in God's opinion. However, when we look at our circumstances, we will tend to see them as potentially harmful to us. But this is a lack of faith based on a wrong perspective: the view of the outward man, not the inward man. The promises of Scripture will not be broken, even to get our attention or to bring us back into fellowship with God. It is simply true that God will not harm us. Once again, we may view it as harm, but God does not. He views it as good for us. We are then safe from harm in all areas.

To this end, whenever we are faced with persecution, we must remember to look at our circumstances "in Christ Jesus." We must view our perceived trouble under the influence of the Holy Spirit. He will always lead us to be at peace, to trust Him, and to have faith in Him and His Word. When we do, we will find ourselves responding to our persecution without a shred of worry.

Do you worry that God may take your spouse or your child? Do you worry that God may take your job or your home? Do you worry about things that if they were to happen, you feel they would bring you great harm? Well then, you are human. I do not mean to suggest that these are not terrible things to endure. I am simply saying if God allows them in your life, they are not going to bring you harm—not in God's eyes. And they won't bring you harm in your eyes, either, if you are living godly in Christ Jesus.

I am not trafficking in unlived examples. I have personally experienced this blessed truth in my life. I have failed to experience it, as well, for the very same reasons listed above. But this one thing is for sure: when we experience such situations, we will find that they produce within us the ability to respond to oppression with another fruit of the Spirit, longsuffering.

I refer to the first three fruits of the Spirit as "inner being transformation" because Romans 12:2 indicates that transformation must come before conformation. We cannot change the way we act until we change the way we think. God must first change the inside of man. The devil begins his work on the outside. He uses outside influences of the lust of the flesh to play on the mind, the lust of the eyes to play on the will, and the pride of life to play on the emotions. The devil's work always begins with outside influence and attempts to destroy us on the inside. God works from the inside out. The inner man is the part of man that communicates with God. The Spirit influences the inner man, and when we yield to that influence, it always conforms the outer being to the image of Christ.

So, if a man does not love or have joy or peace, it can go undetected; it is an inside problem. Before God can get a man to act right on the outside, He must get him to act right on the inside. He offers these three fruits to be the inner man's response to adversity.

Let us now look at the conformation process as we yield to the second three Fruits of the Spirit. I refer to these as "outer-being conformation." They are evidenced by our outward behavior. After a transformation of the mind has begun, these three fruits will cause us to un-conform from the world and conform to the image of Christ.

We Lose Our Freedom to Choose When We Give In to Temptation and Its Consequences. Instead, Make Fruitful Choices for Positive Consequences.

Let the wicked forsake his way, and the unrighteous man his thoughts: and let him return unto the LORD and he will have mercy upon him: and to our God, for he will abundantly pardon. —Isaiah 55:7

Conforming: The Choice between Longsuffering and Being Quick-Tempered

For me, longsuffering is one of the most difficult fruits of the Spirit to yield to. So whenever I do respond to someone with longsuffering, I am certainly aware of the fact that God is doing the work! Longsuffering is "an enduring temperament that expresses itself in patience with the shortcomings of others."

Let's dissect and define this definition. *Temperament* refers to a person's make up, to the passions, attitudes, and other elements of temper that combine to produce a level of irritability, whether high or low. *Enduring* means "to continue without perishing" or "to last long, even to permanence." *Patience* means "calm in temper." Thus, longsuffering is made up of a combination of attitudes that expresses itself in long, lasting calmness. To whom is this combination of attitudes to be expressed? Well, by definition, this spirit of calmness should be expressed toward people who have shortcomings. *Short* meaning "not of sufficient length," and *comings* meaning "to advance toward a target."

I know this is a long explanation of a definition, but I use it to show how God intends for us to respond to those who fail to reach our expected targets. You see, we all have expectations of what other people should be doing and how they should be acting. Too often, we feel let down by people. Whether they are wrong in falling short, or whether our expectations for them are unrealistic, God's intention for us is to always respond with longsuffering. He wants us to respond with an enduring temperament expressed by patience with the shortcomings or faults of others.

Now, let's briefly review the fruit we have studied to this point and notice how each fruit flows out of the previous one. When we love people without thought of return, we experience an absolute rejoicing in all circumstances. This joy leads to freedom from worry in mind, body, and spirit. Therefore, when responding properly to others, we might think that it would naturally yield a great willingness on their part to meet our objectives for them. However, if the devil fails to influence us to react in self-love, frustration, or worry toward people, circumstances, or pursuing pressure, then he will work on others whom he can get to react in a fleshly manner toward us. Satan's goal is to get them to influence us away from the influence of God's Spirit. Satan will do this by swaying them to fall short of our expectations. In other words, the more we do for others, the more they may knowingly or unknowingly let us down.

So, what good does it do for us to respond properly to the needs of the needy, to express joy in difficult circumstances, and to rest in absolute peace in the face of pursuing oppression only to react in a fleshly manner toward those we are trying to help? It makes no sense! Can it be true that the more we allow proper responses to flow through us from the Holy Spirit, the higher our expectations are of those people? The more godly our responses are, the more godly response we expect from others? After all, if we can yield to the Spirit's leading, is it asking too much to demand the same of those who are benefiting from our godly responses to their needs? In a word, yes.

Pastors are in a position to experience this probably more than anyone else. I have heard countless pastors tell how they have helped the hurting in their church. They have done everything they can. They have poured out their hearts in their preaching, in one-on-one counseling, in offering encouragement, and even in providing for personal needs, only to have these same people let them down by leaving without so much as a thank you. Too often they exit the church hurling insults and spewing critical statements, all the while trying to take others with them.

Why does this happen? Well, I believe it is a part of the spiritual warfare that we all face. You see, the devil knows that the best witness is one that is willing to lift up Christ. When Jesus is lifted up, He draws all men unto Himself (John 12:32). When we respond in Christ, under the influence of the Holy Spirit, we bring great glory to God; we make Him look good. This allows the inner man to shine through us unto others. Being an effective witness for our Savior is a great detriment to the devil's kingdom of darkness. Remember, his goal is to keep the gospel hidden from the lost. Second Corinthians 4:3-10 explains how the light shines and how the devil seeks to hide it.

> *But if our gospel be hid, it is hid to them that are lost: In whom the god of this world hath blinded the minds of them which believe not, lest the light of the glorious gospel of Christ, who is the image of God, should shine unto them... For God, who commanded the light to shine out of darkness, hath shined in our hearts, to give the light of the knowledge of the glory of God in the face of Jesus Christ. But we have this treasure in earthen vessels, that the excellency of the power may be of God, and not of us. We are troubled on every side, yet not distressed; we are perplexed, but not in despair; Persecuted, but not forsaken; cast down, but not destroyed; Always bearing about in the body the dying of the Lord Jesus, that the life also of Jesus might be made manifest in our body.*

The devil hides the truth from the lost by blinding their hearts so they cannot see the image of God shining unto them. Anytime people are able to recognize the image of God, it is good news for them. That is why God has created us in His image, so others will see His image in us and thus the gospel shines into the darkness. God helps those who see His light in us to realize His power is in us. Certainly, Christians will go through all kinds of attacks, troubles, disappointments, and persecution, but we can respond to all of this adversity by suffering (for a long time, if necessary) without expressing our disappointment. Our godly response of longsuffering will cause (vs. 10) the light of Christ within us to be made evident to others.

The only way to let our light shine in a dark place is for things to happen to us that will bring attention to the image of Christ within us. Such things may cause us to want to react with fleshly selfishness, frustration, or worry. But if we do, the light of Christ will never shine through. He cannot shine through us unless we allow those circumstances to wound the outer man and let the inner man display the image of God. By rejecting the influence of the Spirit to respond properly, we place a bushel over our candle (Luke 11:33).

Many people believe "putting a candle under a bushel" refers to not being willing to tell people about Christ. That is partly true, but we hide our candle under the bushel of the outer man far more often than by not witnessing. We do so by reacting improperly to difficult circumstances. It is usually our inconsistency in yielding to the Spirit that actually leaves us embarrassed or unwilling to share our faith.

The truth is that no other fruit leads more people to Christ than our yielding to the Spirit's fruit of longsuffering when faced with disappointment in others. As a matter of fact, God's longsuffering toward us was probably a driving force behind our own salvation. His light shone in such a way that we changed our minds from unbelief to belief in Jesus Christ.

> *And thinkest thou this, O man, that judgest them which do such things, and doest the same, that thou shalt escape the judgment of God? Or despisest thou the riches of his goodness and forbearance and longsuffering; not knowing that the goodness of God leadeth thee to repentance?* (Romans 2:3-4)

These verses remind us how easy it is to condemn those who fall short of our expectations. And not only do we judge the weaknesses of others, but we often are guilty of the same shortcomings. By judging them, we show a disrespect for the wealth of goodness, forbearance, and longsuffering of God. We overlook the fact that God's proper responses to our own shortcomings is what led us to repentance.

In other words, God expresses a calm attitude toward our short-comings for long periods of time, and we experience great benefits from that longsuffering attitude. God's longsuffering toward us ought to motivate us to be more willing to respond properly to the shortcomings of others. Satan knows if he can get us to react with a fleshly alternative to longsuffering, less people will repent. The less we respond properly, the less His light will shine from our hearts. If the devil cannot get us to let God down in the face of adversity, then he will get others to let us down in disappointing ways. That is when it is most critical that we respond under the influence of the Spirit to the fruit of longsuffering. To battle against this fruit, the devil has what he considers a more self-satisfying alternative. It is a reactionary work of the flesh, fulfilling the soul's desire to be quick-tempered.

Temper is "a combination of passions that produces a level of irritability or contentment." *Quick-tempered,* then, would indicate that it takes very little or a short amount of irritability to excite our passions in a negative way. Often, a quick temper will be the biggest reason for our unwillingness to share the gospel with others. In my own case, this fear to serve as God was leading was a direct result of the shame of reacting to people with a short temper.

Before I came back to Christ in 1993, I was an incredibly unpro-ductive disappointment to many people who had invested in me. My parents, after ten years of sacrificing for my Christian education, watched with sadness as I went out into the world and rejected a Spirit-led lifestyle. Yet, they always responded in a loving, longsuf-fering way. My employers, seeing great potential in me, over and over again invested in training and preparing me for positions of influ-ence within their organization. Despite their efforts, I never met my potential. To me, their longsuffering spirit toward my shortcomings was nothing more than a form of flattery that led me to take more advantage of them. Eventually, I had a résumé so poor that it left me basically unemployable. Having rejected my Christian upbringing, I set out for a self-satisfying lifestyle that led to drugs, alcohol, and other crippling addictive sinful habits.

Through it all, I received longsuffering responses from God. My list of grievances against my parents, preachers, teachers, employers, and the government was so long that it would be a ridiculous ritual to try to remember them all. Despite it all and the more I transgressed, it seemed the longer that people would suffer for my benefit.

Then came that fateful day when God allowed a near-fatal auto "accident" to open my eyes to the impending judgment of God. As I lay in that hospital bed reading the gospel of John, I came to realize that my shortcomings were costing many people a great deal. I changed my mind, repenting of the way I had perceived the benefits of the many longsuffering responses of those who tried to help me. I began to realize that if I continued to take advantage of the kind gestures of others, God was going to bring my life to an end. He began to work in my heart to establish a healthy fear of the Lord and a genuine spirit of gratitude toward those who were trying to help me.

When I got out of the hospital, my life began to change quickly as a direct result of my repentance and new attitude. I became very productive in my new job, I began to grow in my spiritual life, and in my service to God at church. From that point forward, it just seemed like everything I did went well. It was a very exciting and enjoyable time in my life as I was gaining favor with God and He was giving me favor with man. I went from being one of the most unproductive Christians alive to now being a very productive Christian and full-time servant in the ministry of Reformers Unanimous.

Nevertheless, up until recently I have had one quality about me that nearly everyone who has ever worked under, with, or over me is aware of: being quick-tempered. It was incredibly embarrassing when I came to this realization. It took a lot of bad circumstances in my life to finally break this stubborn lust of my soul to react in a quick-tempered, irritated way to others. Maybe my struggle will open your eyes to a similar situation in your life.

I had spent nearly all my life being unproductive and disappointing nearly everyone in authority over me. When I gave my life back to God, He began to bless me. Seeing the results of my productivity, I increased my expectations of myself, not realizing that the productivity I was experiencing was not a result of me, but of God in me. As I raised my expectations of myself, I also raised my expectations of others. Shamefully, I was not willing to do for others what God had done for me for so long. I became obsessed with attaining spiritual productivity that no one was able to produce at a level that brought me satisfaction.

I expected a level of perfection from my wife and the mother of our children that I was unable to meet myself as a husband and a father. My staff, though working countless hours, was often reprimanded for being unable to get their jobs done or to do them at a standard that I would accept. I became overbearing. I placed heavy and unscriptural burdens on my family, my staff, and our volunteers. These were all fleshly reactions to what I perceived to be the shortcomings of others. Though I had never experienced this fleshly alternative from others when I was failing in every area of my life, I took up this evil temperament of being quick-tempered with those who, I thought, were letting me down. What a sad commentary on a Christian leader!

I did not realize my error for the first three years of my Christian ministry. It wasn't until God led me to write and teach messages on anger that I began to realize I had a very serious problem. I would write the message and study the message, but I could not preach the message. I knew beyond a shadow of a doubt that I would be a hypocrite. I was working hard and so were my staff, but I was disappointed. It brought great discouragement, but I didn't realize the problem until I found myself unable to teach on subjects that God was obviously leading me to teach.

I came to see that I was not expressing a proper temperament toward others. I was putting expectations on them that God was neither putting on them nor on myself. I came to understand that despite the fact that I was quick-tempered with everyone else, God was still being longsuffering toward me. His goodness in response to my badness was very convicting and it led me to repentance.

I have now, to the glory of God, done a 180-degree turnaround in this area. I am not out of the woods when it comes to my fleshly desire to react with my quick temper, but I must say God has given me a great grace to realize my flaw. It wasn't when people quit over the pressure, which people have. It wasn't because people distanced themselves from me, which they did. It wasn't because students felt like under achievers, because I am sure they did, and we probably lost some of them because of it. It was when I realized that, as a result of my fleshly reactions to people's shortcomings, I had hindered God's ability to speak through me on certain subjects. My light was shining less and less. In my zeal to be productive, I became less productive with others.

How about you? Do you have a quick temper with the short-comings of others? If so, it will hinder God's work through you. The devil knows this. If he cannot hinder your productivity by getting you to be selfish, frustrated, or worried, then he will try to lead you to be proud of your God-given productivity. And nothing interferes with the productivity of God like the pride of man.

If you struggle with the being quick-tempered, I encourage you to memorize and meditate on Proverbs 19:11: *The discretion* [proper judgment] *of a man defereth* [delays] *his anger; and it is his glory to pass over* [overlook] *a transgression* [violation].

We need not give in to the temptation to be quick-tempered. If we will use proper judgment, then we can delay our anger with those who let us down. By delaying our anger, we can eventually overlook their violation altogether. Our willingness to let these violations go will make us look good and will in turn make God look good. By yielding to the Spirit, we will always be willing to suffer for a long time with the shortcomings of others. The inner man will flow through, and God will look good as He lives through us.

Conforming: The Choice Between Gentleness and Harshness

The Bible indicates that *gentleness* means "softness in manners." *Softness,* when coupled with *manners,* means "mildness." Our manners are the ways we act in relation to our duties of life, behavior, demeanor, conduct, and management. In other words, *gentleness* means being mild-mannered.

Do you know people who are mild-mannered, whose manners are soft and genteel? Of course we are not talking about having good manners at the dinner table, though that is important. We are talking about a manner of mildness as we face our day-to-day responsibilities. *Mild* means "tender." Thus, a person who is under the influence of the Spirit will act and respond in a tender and mannerly way.

There are people in my life who excel in yielding to a particular fruit of the Spirit. When I think of the fruit of the Spirit Gentleness, I am reminded of my pastor: Dr. Paul Kingsbury is the most gentle man I have ever met. He is mild in every area of his life. Dr. Kingsbury is the father of twelve children. He is the pastor of a church of about a thousand members, the board chairman of Reformers Unanimous International, a husband, and a Christian. He seems to be the busiest man I have ever met. Yet, despite that busyness, he is always joyful, kind, considerate, patient, and willing to listen to anyone who approaches him with a problem.

Recently, I was out of town when I received a call from his daughter Joy, who works for our ministry. She informed me that Joey, her brother, had just been diagnosed with leukemia. This young man had graduated from high school only one month earlier. Joy told me that Pastor Kingsbury was out of town and would be unable to get back for five days.

When he returned home, Dr. Kingsbury was faced with even more tragedy. One of his deacons, a pillar of our church for thirty years, had been diagnosed with cancer and was given only four weeks to live. The following day, a married couple from our church was involved in a motorcycle accident, resulting in the wife's death—a shocking event that rocked our church family! When I arrived home and attended the following Wednesday night's service, most of the congregation were hearing about all three of these situations for the very first time. Oh, how oppressed I felt that evening! But as I watched our pastor lead the service in testimonies and prayer, I was amazed at his gentle manner. I watched him listen intently to so many prayer requests that paled in comparison to the heartaches he was facing. Yet he preached with a soft spirit and with all his heart.

Afterward, I stood in line in the auditorium to speak with Dr Kingsbury As I waited while he talked with the final three people ahead of me, I couldn't help but hear what each of them was talking to him about. I observed as these people brought their seemingly petty problems to him. They appeared to have no regard for the burdens he was carrying on this particular day. Yet the whole time, he looked each person in the eye. He listened and smiled, committing to help and taking notes of things he needed to do to help these members of his flock who were piling more personal problems onto his current load.

Then, when he approached me, he smiled even more broadly. Before I could offer my condolences for the sorrowful circumstances, Dr. Kingsley rushed up to me, gave me a hug, and told me he'd missed me. He then immediately asked me to give him a quick update on all our ministry's problems. Wow, talk about big shoulders! That is a true man of God. How does he do it? Well, he doesn't; God does. When confronted with adversity, he is able to face his responsibilities and conduct himself in a tenderly mannered way. That is God who enables Dr. Kingsley—and you and me—to act and respond to the circumstances of life with the Spirit fruit of gentleness.

I have asked my pastor how he is able to be so mild-mannered toward people. He told me that his ability to respond to his day-to-day duties under the influence of the fruit gentleness is a result of his decision to forgive people for their insensitivities. I have, as a result of his example, learned this lesson as well. You see, I must admit I at times do struggle with these three fruits that deal with conformity of the outer man: longsuffering, gentleness, and goodness.

Some time ago, I started to become abrasive when dealing with my responsibilities of counseling fallen students. I place much effort into each of my students and love them dearly. I struggle when I see them fall, and when they do, I want to help them. However, with some it seems that after they fall, they want to talk about their problems and do nothing about them. I am very careful not to allow my time to be abused by those who are not serious about recovery. I had a few students that were beginning to fall somewhat regularly. I had placed a great deal of time into counseling and teaching them. Over and over again, they would call asking, "Wondered if you have a few minutes?" "Of course I do," was always my reply. When they would arrive, they would give me the news. We would cry, talk, cry, and pray. I would encourage them. It seemed to do no good. Over and over again, they would fall and call. This went on for about five months.

I got to the point that I was anything but gentle in my daily duties. I would come to work discouraged. I would look at my schedule only to see the same names over and over again. To top it off, after some students would fall away and stop asking for help, their slots on my schedule would be replaced by newer students that had been doing well but now were not. Oh, the frustration that I felt! It showed in my mannerisms. My secretary would tell me an appointment had arrived and I would just roll my eyes and think, "Here we go again." I was critical and negative to the repeating offenders. I was harsh and unkind to those that would not follow my counsel quickly and correctly. I was not pleasant to work with and I was not pleasant to counsel with. I did not want a ministry that was steeped in daily devotions of defeat. I wanted our students to only experience a victory that was sustainable and enjoyable. I didn't want the problems that my students were bringing me.

Here is when I realized that *I* had a problem: I was counseling a woman who was bitter at her husband for his continual defeat in his road to recovery. She was mean to him and often unrelenting in her personal criticism of him. I took her to the book of Ephesians to show her how she needed to respond to her husband's failures. While doing so, I realized what was causing me to yield to the fleshly alternative to gentleness. I was struck with conviction and had to excuse myself from our meeting. I asked the Lord to give me the strength to do what these verses say to do. The Bible says to forgive anybody who hurts me, in any way, no matter what they do or how often they do it.

My friend, that is the key ingredient that will release you from the fleshly alternative to gentleness and will allow you to respond in a mild-mannered, tender, and gentle way to your day, your duties, and your disappointments. What was the passage that did this for me? It was Ephesians 4:31-32:

> Let all bitterness, and wrath, and anger, and clamour, and evil speaking, be put away from you, with all malice: And be ye kind one to another, tenderhearted, forgiving one another, even as God for Christ's sake hath forgiven you.

In a previous chapter, I explained the meaning of these verses. However, in review, I would like to look at them again. I think it is important to fully understand how the application of this exhortation can totally change the way we look at our daily duties and our daily disappointments. You see, it is not a sin to be disappointed. It is a sin to allow disappointment to cause you to yield to a lust of the flesh. Let's take a look at the dissected and defined version of these verses on forgiveness.

Bitterness: Compressed feelings
Wrath: Intense desire to get even
Anger: Passions of the mind
Clamour: Argumentativeness
Evil speaking: Gossip
Malice: The desire for another person's physical injury
Kind to one another: An outward demonstration of gentleness
Tenderhearted to one another: An inward demonstration of gentleness
Forgiving one another: An upward demonstration of gentleness

These verses teach us about actions and reactions that are not mild-mannered. In fact, they are just the opposite. These actions and reactions to others or occupations are actually the actions and reactions of another work of the flesh, harshness. Ephesians 4:31-32 explains how most people react to those who they feel are violating them. It is the antithesis of gentleness. If we fight back, tell others off, argue, get violently passionate, attempt revenge, or even suppress our feelings and do nothing about them, then we are not yielding to gentleness. We are exercising the work of harshness.

The dictionary defines *harshness* as "roughness in manner, temper, or words." The desire to do these things can cause us to dislike everybody and everything in our relationships and responsibilities. If we act on these desires, then it will cause others to hate everything about us. Harsh personalities are not enjoyed; they are destroyed. They either self-destruct or are avoided by others and held back from promotion. David said in Psalm 18:35, *Thou hast also given me the shield of thy salvation: and thy right hand hath holden me up, and thy gentleness hath made me great.* Gentleness will lead people to consider you a great person. Harsh people are never considered great guys or great gals.

God wants us to respond in a gentle way when faced with tough decisions. Especially when those decisions are caused by the failure of another. Under His leading, we will always respond gently, never harshly. In James 3:17, we see that when God gives us wisdom in direction, it comes with some uniquely tender responses. *But the wisdom that is from above is first pure, then peaceable, gentle, and easy to be entreated, full of mercy and good fruits, without partiality, and without hypocrisy.*

That's a far cry from my actual reactions to the people who were falling and calling. Was it because I wasn't asking God for help in responding properly? No, my harshness was a direct result of being offended. I was offended that I had worked so hard to help them and yet they were letting me down. I was taking their failures personally and it was destroying my moods and my manners.

That reminds me of another passage I once studied. It is found in 2 Timothy 2:24-26:

> And the servant of the Lord must not strive; but be <u>gentle</u> unto all men, apt to teach, patient, In meekness instructing those that oppose themselves; if God peradventure will give them repentance to the acknowledging of the truth; And that they may recover themselves out of the snare of the devil, who are taken captive by him at his will.

Strive means "to put forth great effort." The Bible is telling us that we should not have to work hard, but rather we need to be apt or willing to teach in a gentle, patient fashion. Surely, to teach in such a genteel fashion without having to work hard, it must be referring to working with people who are easy to work with, people who don't require hard work because they respond well to our gentle and patient teaching. Nope! The next verse says that we need to be willing to teach *those that oppose themselves,* meaning those who do great harm to themselves or those who seem to not care whether they follow our teaching or not. Also, those who need to repent to the truth that we are giving them but often refuse. Such people are snared by the devil and in captivity to him.

Now, I don't know about you, but that seems impossible to me. It would seem these are the people that would need the most effort, the *most* striving. Yet they are not. If we are willing to teach them in a patient and gentle fashion, then we won't have to work hard to keep them. We might even lead them to the position of repentance that will bring them out of captivity!

So, how do we do this? How do we stop trying so hard and instead simply yield to the Spirit's gentleness? By forgiving people in the manner that Paul teaches in Ephesians 4:32. To do this, we must follow his directions. It begins in reverse order of the list. If we start with bitterness, we may never forgive, but if we start with forgiveness, we will never be bitter.

To show an outward demonstration of gentleness, to be kind to one another, we must begin by forgiving the alleged perpetrator. We will never be kind to others until we forgive them. God knows our hearts. If we don't ask Him to give us the grace to forgive them, then we will never receive the benefit of a forgiving heart. That benefit is the second step to responding in a gentle fashion. It will lead us to be tender hearted. If we will forgive them, then we will experience the tender heart we need to continue to the third and final step to responding in a gentle fashion: being kind one to another. That's right. If we forgive others, God will give us tender hearts, and a tender and forgiving heart will be kind to others.

As with every fruit of the Spirit, gentleness is a choice. Let me remind you of Titus 3:1-2: *Put them in mind* [remind them] *to be subject to principalities and powers, to obey magistrates, to be ready to every good work, To speak evil of no man, to be no brawlers, but gentle, shewing all meekness unto all men.*

Conforming: The Choice Between Goodness and Meanness

Some would say the fruit of gentleness is identical to our next response of the inner man, goodness. They would be wrong. Though each fruit does have similarities, they are each different response to different circumstances of life.

Specifically, gentleness is a response from God, but goodness, like love, is an action by God. The Bible indicates that *goodness* is "conforming our lives and conversations to behave benevolently toward others." Goodness is when we allow a conformation, a pouring into a mold, to take place in our lives. The mold that we are being conformed to produces benevolent behavior, both in word and deed. Let's see how that manifests itself in human behavior.

A synonym for *goodness* is *benevolence.* According to Webster's 1868 Dictionary, *benevolent* means "having a disposition to do good; possessing love to mankind, and a desire to promote their prosperity and happiness." Benevolence is a quality of one who is seeking to promote prosperity and happiness in others. That's really the world's definition of a "good" person. For Christians, it's a person who yields to the fruit of the Spirit Goodness. Spirit-led Christians are molded to act and talk in such a way that they promote happiness and prosperity toward everyone. The Bible is full of examples of God's goodness. Let's take a look:

> *Oh how great is thy goodness, which thou hast laid up for them that fear thee; which thou hast wrought for them that trust in thee before the sons of men!* (Psalm 31:19)
>
> *Oh that men would praise the LORD for his goodness, and for his wonderful works to the children of men! For he satisfieth the longing soul, and filleth the hungry soul with goodness* (Psalm 107:8-9).
>
> *And Jethro rejoiced for all the goodness which the LORD had done to Israel, whom he had delivered out of the hand of the Egyptians* (Exodus 18:9).
>
> *And on the three and twentieth day of the seventh month he sent the people away into their tents, glad and merry in heart for the goodness that the LORD had shewed unto David, and to Solomon, and to Israel his people* (2 Chronicles 7:10).

There are so many other verses, both in the Old and New Testaments, that speak of God's unending and undeserved goodness. Do you see how closely related goodness is to the inner man transforming fruit of love? Goodness is actually an outer demonstration of the inner yielding to the fruit of love.

I think one of the best passages that speaks of God's goodness to us is found in Psalm 23.

> *The LORD is my shepherd; I shall not want. He maketh me to lie down in green pastures: he leadeth me beside the still waters. He restoreth my soul: he leadeth*

me in the paths of righteousness for his name's sake. Yea, though I walk through the valley of the shadow of death, I will fear no evil: for thou art with me; thy rod and thy staff they comfort me. Thou preparest a table before me in the presence of mine enemies: thou anointest my head with oil; my cup runneth over. Surely goodness and mercy shall follow me all the days of my life: and I will dwell in the house of the LORD for ever.

Notice David's closing statement. He indirectly points out that this goodness from God is undeserved. Remember, *mercy* is "not getting what we deserve." So David is saying that he doesn't deserve the goodness that he is getting. He is getting it because God is not giving him what he really deserves.

I believe mercy is the primary catalyst for yielding to goodness. Goodness is allied when mercy is applied. It is God's mercy that leads Him to promote happiness and prosperity in our lives despite our failures and frustrations. God's mercy leads Him to be benevolent. Our willingness to yield to the inner man's desire to show love will cause the outer man to conform in behavior to be benevolent. A heart of love produces an action of goodness.

This is what will help people to change their minds about the way they act. When they see goodness demonstrated by others toward them, it leads them to repentance. (Romans 2:4: *...the goodness of God leadeth thee to repentance.*)

This fruit is incredibly evangelistic. Unfortunately, many of us struggle to yield to this fruit, and I believe the reason is because of our unwillingness to offer to others the response of mercy. We often prefer judgment over mercy. God never gives us permission to judge anyone but ourselves! Judgment is reserved for God, not us. We are encouraged throughout Scripture to demonstrate mercy. We are even told to offer grace, giving to people what they don't deserve.

God's command to demonstrate mercy and grace are seemingly tough demands when responding to those who have done us wrong.

But consider: If we are unforgiving, God will be unforgiving; if we do not show mercy, God will not show mercy to us; if we are not willing to give grace to others, God will withhold His grace from us.

One reason we prefer to judge others rather than show mercy is to justify indulging in a fleshly alternative. The obvious fleshly alternative to goodness is meanness. The definition of *mean* is often assumed to be synonymous with *angry, hateful,* or *vengeful.* While those could be attributes of someone who is mean-spirited, that is not the type of meanness I mean.

Meanness is the antithesis of the fruit of the Spirit goodness. It is defined as "refusing to be liberal with charity, thus avoiding any personal expense." These two contrasting types of behavior—being benevolent and being stingy—are often assumed to refer to the giving or hoarding of money. Of course, in a society that is so obsessed with acquiring money, it is understandable if we only think of benevolence and charity as the giving of financial resources. Yet, there is so much more to benevolence than simply giving away money.

For God's work to be done through men, He needs us to demonstrate goodness with our money, time, energies, gifts, and talents, even in our actions and responses to the mistakes of others. God's work is hindered when we act or react to the failures of others refusing to share God's many resources that we have at our disposal. How can we advance the kingdom of God when we focus on the acquisition of and the refusal to expend any valued resource for the sake of the "kingdom of me"?

In Jesus' Sermon on the Mount, He laid out what God thinks about choosing covetousness over benevolence. Take the time to read the whole passage so that you will fully understand our dissecting and defining.

Lay not up for yourselves treasures upon earth,
where moth and rust doth corrupt, and where thieves
break through and steal: But lay up for yourselves
treasures in heaven, where neither moth nor rust doth

corrupt, and where thieves do not break through nor
steal: For where your treasure is, there will your heart
be also. No man can serve two masters: for either he
will hate the one, and love the other; or else he will
hold to the one, and despise the other. Ye cannot serve
God and mammon. Therefore I say unto you, Take
no thought for your life, what ye shall eat, or what ye
shall drink; nor yet for your body, what ye shall put
on. Is not the life more than meat, and the body than
raiment? Behold the fowls of the air: for they sow not,
neither do they reap, nor gather into barns; yet your
heavenly Father feedeth them. Are ye not much better
than they? Which of you by taking thought can add
one cubit unto his stature? And why take ye thought
for raiment? Consider the lilies of the field, how they
grow; they toil not, neither do they spin: And yet I say
unto you, That even Solomon in all his glory was not
arrayed like one of these. Wherefore, if God so clothe
the grass of the field, which to day is, and to morrow
is cast into the oven, shall he not much more clothe
you, O ye of little faith? Therefore take no thought,
saying, What shall we eat? or, What shall we drink?
or, Wherewithal shall we be clothed? (For after all
these things do the Gentiles seek:) for your heavenly
Father knoweth that ye have need of all these things.
But seek ye first the kingdom of God, and his righ-
teousness; and all these things shall be added unto
you. (Matthew 6:19-21, 24-33).

Jesus tells us that we should not focus on the acquisition of temporary things that will be of no value to us when we die. Instead, we should lay up treasures in heaven. The word *treasure* is "a great quantity of anything that is collected for future use." This is the proper focus of life. But Jesus goes even further in telling that we should not worry about accumulating resources for day-to-day living! In our advanced society, that may seem like no big deal, but in those days, that was the central focus of life!

I recently spent seven days in a third world country. In that time, I observed the townspeople as they struggled to survive. My wife and I gained a friendship with a lady who braids the hair of travelers who come to her village. As she spoke to us in broken English, she told of how she begins her days at 8:00 a.m. and finishes at 11:30 p.m., seven days a week. She works over a hundred hours a week! As she was braiding the hair of a young middle-eastern girl and nearing her 11:30 quitting time, her husband walked up to her stand and began placing beads on the little girl's hair to help his wife. He had been at work in the port since 6:00 that morning.

I could not believe that they worked so hard and so long for so little! She told me that they do this to put food on the table for their three pre-teen girls. I was astonished that it took that much effort to provide the basic necessities of food, clothing, and shelter in this impoverished country. Not to acquire more stuff, but to provide week-to-week. Because she can work year-round, she did not need to store up provisions for her family during the winter months. Thus, she and her husband work with a focus only on meeting the basic needs of their family, day by day, week by week.

In Jesus' day, there was not a Wal-Mart in every town. There was no government aid, no unemployment insurance, no welfare, and no return-to-work programs. So, when He told these people to not focus on necessary resources, He seemed to be telling them to abandon their existence! Actually, He was not teaching them to forsake the provision of their daily needs, but rather to get their focus off that and onto the kingdom of God. As we do, God will provide our every need in abundance.

However, it is not enough to merely focus on the kingdom of God. There is another step to having our needs met while here on earth. Jesus says that we must also seek His righteousness. Now what does this mean? Remember, when we do good under the influence of the Spirit, then we are involved in righteousness. Therefore, doing good under the influence of His Spirit is seeking His righteousness. In other words, to gain God's provision, we must experience justification and sanctification. No change in His philosophy here. God's desire is for people to accept Christ's sacrifice and then allow Him to lead them to reach others. Over and over again, Scripture confirms this as God's plan for us. To this end, He offers us goodness, the fruit of the Spirit.

Naturally, the devil tries to suppress this fruit of goodness by frustrating us into focusing on meeting our own needs, thus bumping God out of the equation. If we can meet our own needs, then we will not learn to depend on God.

Just as God's tool of mercy is what creates a desire for Spirit-led believers to respond with a Spirit of goodness to the needy, the devil's tool of meanness is to get flesh-led believers to react to them with judgment. When God would have us give the merciful response of goodness, the devil would have us give the judgmental reaction of meanness.

The primary ministry of Reformers Unanimous International is to impact the lives of the addicted with the Gospel. Of course, as with any ministry, this type of outreach requires benevolence on the part of God's people. To see the lives of the addicted rebuilt, I must do as Nehemiah did when he wanted to rebuild the walls of Jerusalem. I must ask God to meet our every need financially, and then I must petition those whom God has given kingdom wealth to loosen their purse strings. I must request benevolence on the part of God's people.

I enjoy doing this because I get to minister to both the givers and receivers of the benevolence. It is a great privilege because there are often great needs on both sides of a gift. However, sometimes I come across people who are obviously in a position to give, yet their reactions to my requests show undisguised meanness. Let me explain why I believe this happens so often.

I have always been told that working with addicted adults is an incredibly hard ministry to raise benevolence for. I am also told that if I would run a ministry for battered women or underprivileged children, then I would have no problem raising money. No one could justify meanness to such victims. But since I minister mainly to grown adults with self-inflicted problems, many potential givers can justify their meanness That is, they avoid any personal expense by supplanting charity with judgment. They judge the needy to be unworthy of their merciful benevolence, and that is not a right response. It is a sinful reaction. Spirit-led believers should respond in one of two ways: by not giving because God leads them not to give (since He may not give a reason, neither should that person be required to give a reason) or by giving as much as God leads to give, thus yielding to the Spirit-fruit of goodness. By obeying, givers show mercy while laying up treasures in heaven.

Goodness is a choice. Like every other option of the 20 we have and are discussing, it is a choice with consequences only God knows. I don't know about you, but I don't want my treasures consumed by moths and rust and thieves. But distributing benevolence with a heart of mercy to the undeserved, I know I will receive that same mercy back from God, both here and in His kingdom to come. As a child of God you have the fruit of goodness available to you. I would strongly encourage you to use it to benefit others. Let it be said of us even as Paul said of the church in Rome, *And I myself also am persuaded of you, my brethren, that ye also are full of goodness, filled with all knowledge, able also to admonish one another* (Romans 15:14).

Reforming: The Choice Between Faith and Doubt

Our final three fruits of the Spirit deal with what I call "new-being reformation." It should be evident by these final three fruits being observed and yielded to in our lives that we are indeed "new creatures" in Christ (2 Corinthians 5:17).

Every victory in the Christian life is experienced because of the fruit of the Spirit called "faith.". By contrast, every defeat in the

Christian life is experienced because of doubt. We have defined *faith* as "a personal measurement of the level of confidence in what Christ has done and will do in, through, and for us." All Christians have a personal measure of faith, and it should be evident in the life of a Spirit-led believer.

I want you to see that justification is dependent upon faith in information, but sanctification is dependent upon faith in a personal relationship. When Eve responded improperly to the outside influence of the possessed serpent, she did so because she doubted God's goodness to her. She thought God was holding something back and she wanted to know more information about God and being like God. Thus, she ate of the Tree of Knowledge and plunged mankind into utter darkness. Since then, man has set off on a journey to know more about doing good in his own power so he may be like God. Man has rejected a personal relationship for the acquisition of information. To this day, man assumes that knowledge is power, but it is not. Knowing God is power. In the garden, man knew God, but after the fall, man could no longer know God; he could only know *about* God.

To satisfy man's penchant for knowing how to be like God, he was given information in the form of laws, commands, statutes, and judgments. This was to take God's people out of the bondage of barbaric behavior and to civilize them. The purpose of each covenant God made with man was to picture the day when the acquisition of information would become secondary to the development of a personal relationship with Him.

That day came after Christ died and rose again. Since then, man can by faith accept Christ's atonement as payment for his sin, experiencing justification – freedom from the penalty of sin. Believers are new creatures who, though dead, can live in Christ, by faith. Our key verse for this entire book shows us that truth. *I am crucified with Christ: nevertheless I live; yet not I, but Christ liveth in me: and the life which I now live in the flesh I live by the faith of the Son of God, who loved me, and gave himself for me* (Galatians 2:20).

To live this life dead to self and alive in Christ, we must live it by faith. Yielding daily to faith will allow God to work in our lives. This makes us uncomfortable and God's power comes upon us to make us comfortable when we respond in faith—hence the term, Comforter. However, we often run from the leading of faith and cling to the fleshly alternative of doubt. This causes us to make decisions based on information rather than on our personal relationship with God.

Too often, Christians actively doubt the many truths that we have examined throughout this book; truths that have been proven with Scripture and examples of personal experience. Humanly speaking, doubt is easier to rationalize than faith is to internalize. The Bible indicates that *doubt* is "an attitude of unbelief, characterized by rebellion and disobedience toward God." In other words, by choosing to doubt in a given situation, we declare God to be a liar and presume to take control ourselves. You see, the soul can be very convincing, and it always desires to be in control. The soul would rather reject the boundaries of authority and choose instead to indulge in what the flesh thinks, wants or feels. To this end, when we choose to doubt and reject taking the next step of faith led by God, it's because we are yielding to one of the three aspects of the soul.

Some fail to live by faith because they are mind driven. They doubt things because of intellectual reasons. They are thinkers. There are churches that are focused too much on knowing about God because they are led by pastors who are driven by their minds. There are even whole denominations that are intellectually driven.

Another reason some fail to live by faith is because they are emotionally driven. They doubt what they know to be truth because of emotion created by doubt, and the rejection of faith is more pleasing and acceptable to their flesh. There are churches that are focused way too much on emotionalism because they are led by fleshly pastors who are driven by their emotions. There are even whole denominations that are emotionally driven.

The third reason some fail to walk by faith is because they are driven by the desires of their wills. They doubt certain truths because faith may disqualify them from doing what they want or from doing something the way they want to do it. Their will is their master. There are churches that are led by fleshly pastors who are driven by their wills, placing a huge burden on God's laborers and refusing to allow change in any way. There are even whole denominations that are driven by strong-willed leadership.

This is the devil's design not only for God's people in general, but specifically for pastors and church leaders, as well. When God's pastors and our church leaders yield to the lust of doubt individually, their followers will do likewise. When a church is led in the flesh, the members will struggle to yield to faith.

Here is the basic contrast between faith and doubt: When we yield to doubt, we are depending on desire, knowledge, and reasoning to make our decisions; when we yield to faith, we are depending on God through our personal relationship with Him to make our decisions.

This brings me to some final thoughts on the subject of faith. We often ask God to give us more faith. As believers, this is actually an unrealistic request. We have all the faith we need to live the victorious Christian life. The only way to experience the measure of faith that changes our behavior is not to ask God for more faith, but rather to ask God to help us *yield* to the measure of faith that we already have living within us. In looking at the actions and responses of the Holy Spirit, do you consider any of them to be impossible for you to manifest in your life? Do you consider them to be such unlikely choices when faced with the realities of adversity that you reject even the truths themselves? Have you been focused on knowing about God rather than knowing God? If you answered yes to any of these questions, you are being driven by your soul and trying to be like God in your own power. You are using the acquisition of information to justify the failure of your personal relationship. Reject your thoughts, desires, and feelings of doubt, and have faith in the God that took up residence in you. If you do, your faith will bring great power from God – not because you know more *about* Him, but because you know

Him (Daniel 11:32 *the people that do know their God shall be strong, and do exploits.*).

Choose to develop your personal relationship with God by yielding to the fruit of faith. You will then be conforming to His image by allowing the Holy Spirit to do the transforming. However, if you focus your righteousness on the acquisition of information that yields to the work of doubt, then you will be conforming by performing. Performance is never God's design; conformance is. Man performs, God conforms. If you're performing for God, your willingness to yield to faith is weak. Ask God to conform you as you trust and obey, for, as the song goes, there's no other way to be happy in Jesus, but to trust and obey.

Reforming: The Choice Between Meekness and Discord

Meekness is a fruit that is seldom noticed but usually appreciated when applied. Most people probably do not even recognize this fruit unless they were to realize the thought process of the person that is yielding to it. You see, meekness is a fruit that is applied when someone is trying to assist a person who is actually engaged in a work of the flesh. For most of us, meekness is a difficult fruit to yield to.

I have been told that when the translators were interpreting the Greek New Testament into the English language, they could not readily agree on a word that adequately defined the word *praotes*. At first, the closest they could come was the word *weakness,* but that was far from accurately capturing the essence of this Greek word. The true meaning relates to the practice of adding saliva to help someone get a grip on something. For example, if you were to grasp a baseball bat, you might spit into your hands to get a better grip on it. The word literally means "to add a lubricant in order to reduce friction."

So, how is this manifested in Christian character? The word *meekness* means "the ability for God's people to negotiate among others without causing friction." Where is that in our churches? When

God's people respond to each other and to a lost world in the spirit of meekness, it is sure to produce a level of respect and curiosity.

As I mentioned earlier, when I struggle with yielding to a particular fruit, I try to find people who seem to be stronger in yielding to that fruit, someone who exhibits that fruit with apparent ease. I try to learn from them how they attained the grace and faith necessary to become so successful in yielding to that particular fruit.

At a certain point in my secular career, I was promoted to the position of General Manager. It was the first time that I actually had the privilege of managing other people since my re-dedication. In this management position, I soon found out that meekness would be an excellent fruit to master! Unfortunately, yielding to this fruit was just one of life's mysteries to me. However, my employer Dan Arnold, who even now is one of my teachers and counselors, excels in exhibiting this fruit. He is simply the meekest man I have ever met.

Mr. Arnold knows the value of people. He knows they have many weaknesses and understands that each of them has particular strengths that offset their weaknesses. He realizes that if his people's strengths are to ever be a benefit to his organization, he will have to overlook some of those weaknesses. He will have to especially overlook weakness in the area of personality flaws. Most importantly, he realizes how important it is to get a person's co-workers to also overlook those weaknesses of character.

He once told me that there are three things working against the relationships of our people: their weaknesses, our weaknesses, and Satan, who seeks to get us to react to each other's weaknesses improperly. In other words, we have very little chance that people will just naturally get along. These relationships require a spiritual man to add a lubricant to reduce the friction. Dan realizes the value of helping people get along with one another for the sake of keeping the "working family" together. His organization is very much like a family, and he is truly loyal to his people. He does not want to see them leave the organization, especially over personality weaknesses that could be improved with time.

He once told me that the key to running a successful organization is to develop people daily. He has that slogan on a tab in his day planner, and he moves that tab forward every day. His goal is to always utilize people's strengths, but not stop there. He also works diligently to help them overcome their weaknesses.

However, his ways were not my ways. I did it quite differently. When I would see a weakness in someone, I would "share" it with them. I would give them flack for it and often "encourage" them to shape up in that area. I actually created more controversy than their weakness ever created. I caused a lot of friction with my leadership style. But I knew of no other way.

So, I watched Mr. Arnold and I saw a different type of "people development" going on. I would observe him as he would discuss something with someone who was frustrated with another staff member. He would never criticize the weaker employee to the person who was complaining. Actually, he would try to explain why that person may have acted the way he did and would encourage the complaining employee to be patient and to overlook the mistake.

Then, in a day or so, he would work with the person with the weakness, not deriding him or telling him how much trouble he was causing with the other staff member. Rather, he complimented him on his areas of strength. Dan would then give that person work assignments that were well thought out. They were tasks that would expose that employee's weakness to himself. Dan would be right there to encourage and advise as necessary. Not only that, he would also point out to the weaker employee the strengths of the person who had complained, as an encouragement to both employees.

This type of leadership produces a wonderful spirit of "people development" in the workplace. It took me years to even understand what was happening. Only recently was I able to even define it, much less apply it to my own "people development" skills. Some would call Dan Arnold a "flat liner." Nothing gets him excited. He is neither emotionally up or down, no matter what type of people-failure he's facing.

Why is meekness so valuable in our professional lives (as well as in our relationships with God's people)? As Mr. Arnold pointed out, we have three things working against us: their weaknesses, our weaknesses, and Satan himself. Without our willingness to yield to the fruit of meekness, we will never apply the lubricant necessary to get along with our co-workers or our co-laborers in Christ. Plus, the burden lies on us to get along with *all* people. How else will we be called upon during their times of great need? How else can we show them the love of God in the face of affliction? Let's take a look at the biblical role we have when faced with a weakness on the part of a fellow believer.

> *Brethren, if a man be overtaken in a fault, ye which are spiritual, restore such an one in the spirit of meekness; considering thyself, lest thou also be tempted. Bear ye one another's burdens, and so fulfil the law of Christ. For if a man think himself to be something, when he is nothing, he deceiveth himself* (Galatians 6:1-3).

This passage gives us the biblical precept for restoration of an erring Christian—to restore him to his former standing in fellowship with Christ using the spirit of meekness. When someone's personal weakness is made evident to us, we should begin a healing and repairing process. This does not mandate a public proclamation of that person's sin. What Paul is telling us here is that when someone steps forward with a fault, we should restore that person in a way that doesn't cause friction! If we don't, then we ourselves may face similar situations that could cause us to be overtaken. Our fall will surely be met with the same discord that we applied to those who needed our spirit of meekness.

God's people should always be willing to encourage others in a way that reduces friction. That means we cannot just say what we feel like saying to those who have glaringly obvious personality flaws.

Doing so would not be exhibiting the fruit of meekness. And if *meekness* means getting along with people without causing friction, then the opposite would be not getting along with people by *causing* friction. This is *discord,* another work of the flesh.

As the leader of a ministry that produces adult converts, I have seen the damage done by discord. It can bring great harm to a baby believer, and that is the devil's design. I have heard it said many times that the Christian army is the only one that shoots its own wounded. I don't want to believe that saying, but, as is often the case with such clichés, there is some truth to it.

Discord is one of the most damaging works of the flesh that we have studied. Webster's 1828 Dictionary defines *discord* as "any disagreement which produces angry passions, contest, disputes, litigation, or war." Discord may exist in any relationship. Problems have been in families since Cain and Abel. It is no wonder that they permeate our church families, as well.

Let's look at the words of James, one of the Bible's best educators on human behavior, to see what he says about the value of meekness and the dangers of discord. After giving several illustrations of what great damage can be done by the tongue, James offers this cure:

> *Who is a wise man and endued with knowledge among you? let him shew out of a good conversation his works with meekness of wisdom. But if ye have bitter envying and strife in your hearts, glory not, and lie not against the truth. This wisdom descendeth not from above, but is earthly, sensual, devilish. For where envying and strife is, there is confusion and every evil work. But the wisdom that is from above is first pure, then peaceable, gentle, and easy to be intreated, full of mercy and good fruits, without partiality, and without hypocrisy. And the fruit of righteousness is sown in peace of them that make peace* (James 3:13-18).

It is the job of wise and knowledgeable teachers to teach others with meekness how to live right by example. The teacher, because he has the works to back up the words, can explain to believers that busybody conduct is not from God, but is devilish and sensual (that is to say, it stimulates certain senses of our emotions). Without this type of leader in the church working with our tongue troubles, then we will experience confusion and evil work within the body of Christ. God doesn't create confusion, the devil does! Verse 17 explains the sweet spirit that God will send to permeate the church if the people will invest in opportunities to make peace whenever possible.

This type of leadership would yield wonderful results. Anything short of having a "tongue police" within our church would be of great value! However, I think a good way to apply this truth would be to have someone within the church train others. This teacher should be someone who has proven himself to be exceptional at yielding to the fruit of the meekness. The lessons would include how to develop faith, grace, and obedience in learning to yield to the fruit of meekness. It could save a lot of problems in our churches.

In my opinion, my home church, North Love Baptist Church in Rockford, IL, is one of the meekest churches in America. Yet, it was not always that way. God used our pastor to foster such an atmosphere because God knew He needed an environment at our church that was conducive for baby Christians to grow; for surely, God intended to send many of them our way.

When Reformers Unanimous first began in 1996, I had a student who, for the sake of her privacy, I will call "Joan." Joan attended class nearly every Friday for six months. She seldom missed. However, no matter how many times my wife and I invited her to church, she would kindly respond, "No, thanks." I knew she was not attending church anywhere else, so one day I asked why she would not even try to attend our church. She explained that she did not have a dress and she was waiting to save up enough money to buy one. Then she would attend. I explained to her that she did not have to wear a dress to attend our church; she could wear her nicest outfit and no one would say anything to her. She agreed that she could, but insisted that she wanted to have something special to wear the first time she went to church. Being impressed with her desire to give God her best, my wife and I offered to buy her a dress, but she refused. "God wants me to buy it myself!" Well, out of ammunition, I surrendered.

About six weeks later, Joan exclaimed to me with gladness that she had saved enough money to buy a dress. She would be at church the following Sunday. My wife and I were overjoyed. That Sunday, when Sunday school dismissed, Lori and I anxiously headed upstairs to meet Joan. When we got to the top of the stairs, we saw Joan hanging her coat up. As I turned the corner toward her, my heart sank. She had purchased a very short mini skirt. I sympathetically thought to myself, "She doesn't know any better." So, we told her we were so glad to see her and welcomed her to our church. We took her to our usual seats near the front of the church. Everyone was kind to Joan, and she received no stares or glares for her "way-too-short" skirt. As the choir walked onto the platform, Joan began to realize that her choice of dress was not like what the other Christian ladies were wearing. She tugged on the hem of her skirt, trying to bring it toward her knees. She was uncomfortable but that was okay. She was still observing and learning. I knew her heart was in the right place.

After the service, however, things went downhill fast. As I was talking with someone else, Joan was approached by one of our church's "finest." This wonderful woman took it upon herself to inform Joan of the inappropriateness of her clothing. She exclaimed how her husband "could not keep his eyes off your nakedness" during the service and chided her on her rebellion of indecency in the house of God. Joan fled in tears. She has never been back to class or our church since then.

Indeed, several situations like this happened in the early days of the RU ministry. In hindsight, it was a necessary period in our church's history. It was especially challenging for me. But, these types of situations, coupled with what I was learning at work from Mr. Arnold, taught me the value of being a leader who yields to the fruit of the meekness. To be effective at work and in ministry, I had to learn to submit to the Holy Spirit's direction to reduce friction between people.

When I told my pastor about Joan's experience, he was absolutely heartbroken. Immediately, his preaching shifted toward what we see in James 3. He drew on his own experiences of taming his tongue and began to teach others how to as well. Within a short time, the very spirit and atmosphere of North Love Baptist Church changed. Since that time, it has become fertile soil for baby fruit to grow, developing to incredible levels of maturity beyond what many might find possible to experience in most churches today. Why? Because a wise man, our pastor, with knowledge showed others how it ought to be done. If we are going to destroy discord, we must teach ourselves to restrain our tongues. We must choose to yield to the Spirit's leading to achieve the consequence of reducing friction between others. And finally, we must take what we have learned and teach it to others. As Mr. Arnold taught me, we must develop people daily!

Reforming: The Choice Between Temperance and Self-Indulgence

As we near the end of our study of the fruit of the Spirit, we find a fruit that some think should be mentioned first. But under the influence of the Spirit, Paul listed it last—not because it is the least of all the fruits, but because it is the completion of all the fruits. It takes temperance to put us into a position of being Spirit-led believers. Temperance is essential to keep the passions of the mind, will, and emotions suppressed, allowing the Holy Spirit to rule our lives.

When questioned on the definition of temperance, many people would describe it as "self-control." Even children's songs teach the value of temperance and define it as "self-control." Nothing could be further from the truth! We have seen in so many lessons throughout this book that we ought never to be in control of ourselves. Actually, "self-control" is an oxymoron. There is nothing about me that I can control that will gain God's acceptance of me. I must stop trying to control myself. The more I control myself, the less God is in control of me. Thus, the true definition of *temperance* is Spirit-control or, more specifically, "Spirit-controlled in all of life's pleasures."

Life as given by God offers many pleasures. However, the devil seeks to take those pleasures and turn them into objects of lusts. His goal is to get us to enjoy all of God's pleasures in a lustful way, creating appetites that are ungodly and out of control. The absence of Spirit-control is the single most fleshly action that produces habitual sins.

To fully enjoy the benefits God offers, we must yield to the fruit of the temperance. Many Christians fail to cultivate this fruit, opting rather to reject most of life's pleasures in an attempt to control the temptation to fuel fleshly lusts. I believe this leads God's people into spiritual bondage, otherwise called legalism. True, legalism is the belief that people can get to heaven by doing good works. Though Christians do not believe this, we tend to strive toward obtaining a level of righteousness in our own power that ultimately makes us self-righteous. I call this "legalistic sanctification." As I have mentioned before, we readily accept that justification that comes by God doing all the work, but when it comes to sanctification, we act as if we need to row our own canoe. We believe we need to help God out.

This is a mistake in Christian development. Although we avoid the obviously unrighteous sins listed in Galatians 5:19-21, we still find ourselves over indulging in the natural affections of the flesh. This leads to discouragement and frustration in the Christian life, so we try hard to do better. We serve until we're half-dead, but we receive little joy in return. So the mind, will, and emotions begin to tell us that our lack of joy is due to not acting righteously enough, and that failure is because we are allowing ourselves to enjoy too many of life's pleasures. To compensate, we reject all forms of enjoyment to try to please God, much like a monk tries to gain God's favor through abstinence. This is a perversion of God's designed intention of pleasure.

Admittedly, then we should avoid situations that could lead us to compromise our Christian walk. Nevertheless, we must be willing to allow God to put us into circumstances that will permit us to yield to the fruit of temperance. When we do so, God is in control of the pleasures of life and His Spirit can monitor our enjoyment of them. I know people who refuse to own a television. They will not eat any food that might be nutritionally weak. They will not go to a fireworks show in the City Square on Independence Day. They will hide in their basements with all the lights out on Halloween (which might not be that bad of an idea). They will not permit their kids to play organized sports. They will not go to the mall. They will rip out pages from magazines before their husbands can see them; and many, many more things that are done to prevent themselves or those they care about from being tempted.

Now, before you start thinking that I feel it is acceptable to carelessly place yourself or those you love in harm's way, please notice the context of my statements. This entire book was written in such a way as to prove that I am a strong proponent of avoiding the snares of the devil. However, God wants us to endure temptation. It is His design. Remember when Jesus fasted for forty days in the wilderness? The Bible says He was led there by the Spirit to be tempted by the devil himself (Matthew 14). Jesus taught us that when we pray, we ought to ask God to not lead us into temptation. How could we request such a thing if God is not in control of whether or not we must endure temptations?

To be sure, God wants to develop our souls to yield to the inner man's leading of temperance. God wants us to be under His control in the unpleasurable circumstances of life as well as in all the pleasurable circumstances of life. The only way to avoid temptation completely is to sever your relationship with the outside world, and many religions require just that. However, we cannot do that and function in society, much less be effective in evangelism. So the devil will try to get us to give up all interaction with the pleasures of life and to do good in our own power. Then, as we are performing instead of transforming, he will place an incredibly appealing temptation in our way, and overcoming it in our own power will not be enough to sustain victory. We will eventually indulge in our fleshly desire because it is impossible to endure the temptations of the devil indefinitely in our own power. We are no match for Satan without the power of God.

We will remain crippled in our evangelistic outreach if we avoid any interaction with this world. Being laden with hidden desires and secret sins that make us feel dirty and defeated is spiritual bondage. It is the soul of man controlling the spirit of man.

God has a better way. His plan is for us to face temptation with the confidence of knowing that He has provided a way of escape. That way of escape is revealed by the inner man. God, communicating by His Spirit, will enable us to walk away from a pleasure temporarily or to abstain from it all together. When we allow this type of spiritual interaction between the soul and spirit to take place, we are exercising our faith. It will grow and strengthen just like a muscle. It is called spiritual development. It means giving every bad thing and every good thing to God, staying under His control in all things.

Let's revisit some verses in Romans that help explain God's demands for abstinence from sinful behavior.

- As a result of God's work on our behalf, sin should be decreasing in our lives, not increasing.
  What shall we say then? Shall we continue in sin, that grace may abound? God forbid. How shall we, that are dead to sin, live any longer therein? (Romans 6:1-2)
- God destroyed the power that sin had over us so that we could serve someone other than self. This someone that we would serve (through submission to His leading) will bring us freedom.
  Knowing this, that our old man is crucified with him, that the body of sin might be destroyed, that henceforth we should not serve sin. For he that is dead is freed from sin (Romans 6:6-7).

- God does not want us to yield to those old desires anymore. The power is gone, but the desire is still there. To destroy the desire, we must yield to God's power in our life.

  Let not sin therefore reign in your mortal body, that ye should obey it in the lusts thereof. Neither yield ye your members as instruments of unrighteousness unto sin: but yield yourselves unto God, as those that are alive from the dead, and your members as instruments of righteousness unto God. For sin shall not have dominion over you: for ye are not under the law, but under grace (Romans 6:12-14).

- If we indulge fleshly appetites, they will grow stronger. If we feed our Spirit-led appetites, they will grow stronger, as well. Be careful! God will never feed a fleshly appetite, but we will – after we tire of performing in our own power.

  Know ye not, that to whom ye yield yourselves servants to obey, his servants ye are to whom ye obey; whether of sin unto death, or of obedience unto righteousness? Being then made free from sin, ye became the servants of righteousness (Romans 6:16,18).

So, we could never justify willfully placing ourselves in harm's way, making it harder for us to avoid sin. Certainly, God is against feeding our sinful appetites. But, we equally need to guard against placing ourselves in positions conducive to developing the outer man's self-righteous lifestyle. Allowing this form of self-development hinders God's work on our behalf. Friend, our Heavenly Father will rip the cover off of your self-righteous behavior, and I would hate to see what He will permit you to endure in your own power, eventually bringing about a much-needed lesson in your life. For whom the Lord loves, He most certainly chastens.

Rather than utterly rejecting my view on Spirit-control of life's pleasures versus self-control consider the following conclusion: If we control life's pleasures, then life's pleasures will control us; but, if God controls our pleasures, then we will be safe from harm in the face of temptation, because His plan includes our way of escape.

The reason that soul-control, or what people refer to as self-control, is often taught in our churches is because when we are weak spiritually, we will reject the fruit of the Spirit-Temperance and instead engage in the work of self-indulgence. So, to offset spiritual weakness as church members, many people assume it is best for us to learn how to control ourselves. Then, if we reject God's control, we can fall back on our own control and not engage in sinful self-indulgence. But remember when we try to control ourselves, it is just the flesh trying to control the flesh. It's not the flesh of self-indulgence, but good flesh is just as bad as bad flesh. Therefore, self-indulgence is when self control ceases to control itself. We will lose the battle of spiritual warfare when we indulge appetites on a regular basis, hindering our spiritual walk.

To help illustrate the difference between temperance and self-indulgence, I'd like to present an explanation of appetites. Appetites are the determining factor in every good or bad decision that we make. There are basically three types of appetites in life. Let's take a look.

Some appetites need to be satisfied. These are good appetites. Most people do not naturally have appetites for things that are good. To gain good appetites, we must determine what creates those appetites and then feed them. Feeding them will temporarily satisfy them. It is good for them to be satisfied. The reason that they do not remain that way is good, as well. You see, if they remained satisfied, we would never need to feed them again. As a result, we would lose our appetite for that which is good. Thus, when we feed a good appetite, it will become temporarily satisfied, causing our good appetite to grow. As it grows, so does the necessity for feeding it. Consequently, good appetites should never be over-fed or starved, but rather should be fed on a regularly scheduled basis.

Some examples of good appetites that need to be created and fed are a daily "God and I" time, church attendance, serving, soul winning, family time, work ethics, nutritional food, physical exercise, etc. Notice Matthew 5:6. *Blessed are they which do hunger and thirst after righteousness: for they shall be filled.* This verse tells us that God will completely provide for our yearning to yield to the inner man (i.e., righteousness). Obviously, these are appetites that must be regularly filled or else the cares of this world will eventually draw us dry. However, Jesus assures us that whenever we seek to be filled with the Spirit's leading, we will always be fed by God. Such an appetite will lead us to even greater blessings.

Some appetites need to be starved. These are the appetites that are sinful and should not be fed at any time. These appetites will grow to be insatiable with just the slightest feeding. They are small appetites that require little food to grow; a look here, a thought there; a point there and a click here. If we indulge these appetites, they will quickly control us. They are never fully satisfied and always require more feeding to keep them alive. When they want to be fed, they will bring us nagging misery as they attack our minds.

Examples of these appetites include the sins listed in our key passage in Galatians 5, as well as the sins of our fleshly works (i.e., the alternatives to the fruit of the Spirit.) Other examples may involve drugs, alcohol, gambling, pornography, anger, pride, or possession-centeredness. Still, other examples may look right but are equally wrong such as self-love, frustration, worry, doubt, etc. These behaviors must be strictly avoided. If you have a problem in any of these areas, follow RU Principle number four to protect yourself, and then develop your inner man to reject these sinful, insatiable appetites of the soul. They will destroy your life sooner rather than later.

Let's look at what the Bible says about the dangers and disappointments of feeding appetites that God intends for us to starve.

> *All the labour of man is for his mouth, and yet the appetite is not filled. Better is the sight of the eyes than the wandering of the desire: this is also vanity and vexation of spirit* (Ecclesiastes 6:7, 9).
> *He that loveth silver shall not be satisfied with silver; nor he that loveth abundance with increase: this is also vanity. When goods*

increase, they are increased that eat them: and what good is there to the owners thereof, saving the beholding of them with their eyes? (Ecclesiastes 5:10-11)
And have no fellowship with the unfruitful works of darkness, but rather reprove them. For it is a shame even to speak of those things which are done of them in secret (Ephesians 5:11-12).

These verses remind us that all of our efforts to satisfy our wrong desires will be to no avail. Whether we get what our appetite desires or whether it is withheld from us, we will not be satisfied with the consequences of these appetites either way.

Some appetites need to be suppressed. Each of the three appetites listed requires us to yield to the fruit of temperance to feed, starve, or suppress as needed. This third type of appetite is for those things which God gave us a natural need, drive, or use for and intended for our good pleasure, but these appetites, when indulged in with abandon will lead to lusts that will eventually control us. These are good, yet potentially dangerous appetites of the soul which the inner man will monitor as we yield to temperance. Abuse of these appetites will probably not destroy your life sooner but if fed without temperance, they will destroy your life later.

Once again, these appetites are not designed by God to generate sinful behavior. They are God-given appetites. Actually, many of them are a necessity to live, yet they can still lead to great bondage if we are not careful. Examples of these appetites that must be suppressed from controlling us are for things like food, sleep, relaxation, possessions, money, sexual relations with your spouse, work, play, sports, news/talk radio, television, reading, etc.

In 1 Corinthians 6:12, Paul speaks of these appetites. *All things are lawful unto me, but all things are not expedient: all things are lawful for me, but I will not be brought under the power of any.* He realized the importance of controlling good appetites and was careful to do so. He did not feed appetites that were not beneficial. He starved appetites that would be considered fleshly. Why?

Because he refused to be the servant of anything other than the Spirit of God.

Remember, control over these appetites will require an effort on our part. Not effort to do the work ourselves, but rather an effort to allow God to do the work for us. Temperance is just that – being under the control of the Spirit. Appetite control will require a putting off of the old man and a putting on of our Lord Jesus Christ. *But put ye on the Lord Jesus Christ, and make not provision for the flesh, to fulfill the lusts thereof* (Romans 13:14).

In every life situation, we can make choices that will allow the fruit of the Spirit to grow in us. Against these "fruitful" choices there is no law (Galatians 5:23), and the consequences of such choices honor God and bless those around us.

God Balances Guilt with Blame. Accept the Blame for Your Actions and God Will Remove the Guilt.

If we confess our sins, He is faithful and just to forgive us our sins, and to cleanse us from all unrighteousness.

—1 John 1:9

As a young man trying to get away from the strong-holds of my addictions, I sought the counsel and help of people in secular programs. Time and time again they searched for hidden meaning in my behavior. They explained how my rebellion and desire to please myself was most assuredly to be blamed on my parents and that I had been forced into my sin by what they referred to as bad surroundings. Many in society today are teaching us to shift the blame for our shortcomings on our parents, our upbringing, our economic background, our race, our minority status, and many other things. By shifting the blame to others, it temporarily removes the guilt.

You see, God designed us with a spiritual equilibrium. When we commit sin, we experience guilt and it throws our spirit off-balance with our emotions. When society teaches us to shift the blame (or if we naturally shift the blame), we actually can circumvent that off-balance feeling of guilt temporarily. However, when the sin returns, the guilt is so much worse. Our feelings of failure rise to even higher levels. God's design is to administer guilt through His Spirit who lives within the believer. That guilt needs to be released, and God designed a formula for that to happen. It is found in 1 John 1:9: *If we confess our sins, He is faithful and just to forgive us our sins, and to cleanse us from all unrighteousness.* What a beautiful promise! *If* is a big word. If we do, He will. If we don't, He won't! If we confess [proclaim to God] our sin, He is faithful [for sure, 100 percent of the time, over and over again] to forgive [fully pardon] our sins. He doesn't stop there. You see, we have been pardoned for our wrongdoing, but we are not cleansed from it. We still have the guilty feeling. We must be cleansed of all unrighteousness.

If my daughter got dressed for Sunday school and then went outside and fell in the mud, I would not only forgive her for playing outside when it was raining and she was dressed for Sunday school, I would also clean her. I would give her a bath and all new clothes. Why? Because when I bring her to Sunday school, I don't want anyone to know that she fell in the mud! That is what God wants to do for us. He wants to give us a full pardon for everything we've done in the past, and He wants to clean us up and give us a new set of clothes. And He is faithful! That means He wants to do this every time we sin against Him. He loves us that much. So, today, accept the blame for what you have done in your life. Confess it to God, and know that He will clean you up. Praise God!

God's Mercy to a Wayward Child: Me

In 1993 I had a near-fatal car wreck. My story is quite an amazing testimony of God's mercy toward a wayward child. While in the hospital bed, and after ten years of rebellion against God, I was searching for some answers. One of my former Christian schoolteachers visited me and encouraged me to read the Bible while in the hospital. I decided to take his advice and asked my nurse for a Bible. She reached into the dresser drawer and pulled out a King James Version Bible that had been placed there by an organization called "Gideons International." I appreciated their ministry that day, as I used that Bible to light my way [course of life] back to the local church of my youth.

Even though my parents had sacrificed for me to receive a sound Christian education, I had refused the wisdom of God. My parents brought me up in a godly home, but I would not even listen to them, much less obey them. Teachers and employers had seen potential in me, but I refused their counsel. I was addicted to drugs and alcohol. I was only concerned about my own pleasure.

On that hospital bed, I came to grips with the fact that there was absolutely no one else to blame for my state in life but myself. I was unclean before God. I soon discovered that another word for unclean is *guilty*. When God calls someone unclean, He is calling him or her guilty. God's Spirit is without sin. He has no guilt and produces no guilt or condemnation. But in the dark spirit world of the devil, all are guilty under sin.

The New Testament contains the word *unclean* thirty times. In twenty of those instances, it is used in reference to demonic spirits.

The other ten times refer to things which were unholy according to Old Testament Law. So, we can see that being unclean is something God considers evil or under the influence of evil.

Yet I also discovered that, as believers, we cannot be unclean. We are not guilty of anything any longer. We are forgiven for everything and we will receive no condemnation for what we have done. In Acts 10:9-16, Peter has a vision and hears God's voice: *And the voice spake unto him again the second time, What God hath cleansed, that call not thou common.* The word *common* means "defiled." The animals mentioned in this passage are symbolic not of unclean spirits, but of people formerly under demonic possession, or unclean [guilty]. Since God has cleansed us, we cannot be defiled by an indwelling demonic spirit. We have been cleansed. First John 1:7 tells us, *the blood of Jesus Christ his Son cleanseth us from all sin.*

Titus 1:15 says, *Unto the pure all things are pure: but unto them that are defiled and unbelieving is nothing pure; but even their mind and conscience is defiled.* The "defiled" are those who are unbelievers. The believers are those who are now pure. First John 3:2-3 reminds us that we are children of God. Though at times we don't appear to be like Him, when He returns, we will be just like Him. He says in verse 3 that those who have this hope in Him keep themselves pure:

> *Beloved, now are we the sons of God, and it doth not yet appear what we shall be: but we know that, when he shall appear, we shall be like him; for we shall see him as he is. And every man that hath this hope in him purifieth himself, even as he is pure.*

Now, realizing that we are pure and that God sees us as cleansed by the blood of our Lord Jesus, let's look at how the devil can influence us to live as if we were back in bondage and unclean. He cannot make us unclean, but if he can get us to act unclean, we will feel unclean. We can behave as if we were possessed, but the truth is that we are being oppressed and yielding to the oppression.

Earlier we discussed friendships that could be considered bad influences. The key verse was 2 Corinthians 6:14. Paul tells us in this verse not to be unequally yoked. He compared this partnership to light and darkness – God's influence partnering with evil influences. Verse 15 continues on to explain that Christ and Satan have no harmony [concord] together, no partnership whatsoever; no positive interaction. They agree on nothing (vs 16). We are His temple and He lives in us. Verse 17 then tells us to come out and separate ourselves from these types of influences that are not in agreement with our inner influence. And then in 2 Corinthians 7:1, we are given the following responsibility: *Having therefore these promises, dearly beloved, let us cleanse ourselves from all filthiness of the flesh and spirit, perfecting holiness in the fear of God.*

This appears to be a request for us to *do* something that will cleanse us. We know that all efforts in our own power to establish a form of righteousness is of no good. So what work is Paul referring to? If we are already clean, then why do we need to cleanse ourselves? Well, in God's eyes, we *are* clean. But that does not mean we act, think, or feel clean. The truth is, we are clean in spite of how we feel. This verse is not talking about our cleanness in our position with God, but rather in our position with man. God can see us as clean, but the world, based on our behavior, can see us as unclean. Paul called it "the filthiness of the flesh and the spirit." Now, that is an odd criticism – calling the spirit unclean. But that is not what this verse means. He is calling "the flesh and the spirit" unclean. Let me explain with a short review from previous chapters on the flesh and the spirit.

The **soul** is the outer man: your mind, will and emotions.
The **spirit** is the inner man: God's mind, will, and emotions in us.
The **flesh** is the members [body parts] that are under the influence of the soul.

When we walk "after the flesh," we are taking repeated steps under the influence of the outer man. This is our way of thinking, wanting, and feeling. When we walk "in the Spirit," we are taking repeated steps under the influence of the inner man. This is God's way of thinking, wanting, and feeling, manifested as Christ living not only in us, but also through us.

If a person is engaging in drugs or alcohol, then we understand that to be flesh. He is doing what he wants and definitely not what God wants. That is easy to define as flesh. It is unrighteous flesh. However, there is another flesh that hardly anyone knows about. It is not unrighteous flesh, and there is no such thing as righteous flesh, so what other type of flesh could there be? Self-righteous flesh. That's right, acting righteous in our own power. Despite the fact that we have been cleansed by God's power, we try to act clean in our own power rather than the power of God. No wonder we still feel the guilt of the flesh!

Now, how might that flesh – the flesh of self-righteousness – appear? Here are some examples:

A person gives $45 every week in the offering plate on Sunday morning as his tithe. The person never fails to give this offering.

A person mows his pastor's lawn every week, without fail, for free.

A person sings in the church choir and also sings solos.

A person teaches Sunday school.

The list can go on and on. How could we do these things that seem so good, yet do them "after the flesh" rather than "in the Spirit"? It's simple. Often, we actually begin by doing them in the Spirit, but then end up doing them "after the flesh" in our own power. Paul warned the church of Galatia about this in Galatians 3:3. *Are ye so foolish? having begun in the Spirit, are ye now made perfect by the flesh?* This is what the outside oppression of the devil can do to believers. The devil has no power within. The only powers within a believer are the power of God and the power of man living together, preferably with the power of man submitting to the power of God. However, the commanding forces of the devil will place outside influences that are oppressive on us to get the power of man to run the Christian life. When we do This, we will appear clean to man, but under the conviction of the Holy Spirit, we will not feel clean. It makes us feel discouraged and fleshly. Because we are! Let's look more closely at our examples to see how this can happen.

A person gives $45 every week as his tithe. But through the years, his income has grown from $450 per week to $600 per week. This person is not a giver; he is a robber. He is doing good (by putting money in the offering), but he is doing it in the power of the flesh.

A person mows his pastor's lawn every week. He doesn't expect his pastor to give him money, but if his pastor doesn't thank him regularly and even sometimes from the pulpit, he gets offended and quits. That's not love, the fruit of the Spirit; it is the lust of the flesh, self-love.

A person sings in the church choir and also sings solos. She used to beg God for His power to use her gift, but now she hardly practices because she has learned to "perform" in her own power. She doesn't need God's power because she has gotten good enough to sing in her own power.

A person teaches a Sunday school class. He used to beg God for His direction in what to teach and for the power to teach it. But now, after a number of years, he doesn't look for God's direction or power. As a matter of fact, he waits until Saturday evening around 9:00 p.m., struts over to the computer to string a few thoughts together and get a few clean jokes off the internet, and off he goes. By starting class late and adding a few "illustrations," he might even turn it into a two-week lesson. What is he doing? A good work, but in the power of his flesh.

Now, be sure of this, no one else may ever know it, but people such as these will feel unclean. They will not experience the fruit, or outcome, of the Spirit. Their work is not an outcome of the Spirit; it is an outcome of the flesh. (In parts a and b of chapter 9, I explain the differences between them more thoroughly.) These Christians will not experience joy but, rather, frustration in their work and walk.

That is what the filthiness of the flesh and spirit is in 2 Corinthians 7:1. It is when someone who is indwelled by the Spirit allows himself to be led by the flesh to do "good things." It is when the flesh tries to imitate the Spirit. We often do not realize it, but it is why we get so frustrated in the work of the Lord.

The truth is that when we engage in self-righteous flesh long enough, our frustration will cause us to lower our guard, and that same evil influence will oppress us into unrighteous flesh. The result is doing something in our flesh that is wicked and was once unthinkable. That is the purpose of the oppression – to get us to act in our own power, rather than yielding to God's power within us. Eventually, we will live under the power of the oppressor. Possessed? No, not possible. But oppressed. We will begin to act unclean. Under this influence, we will first *think* unclean, then *act* unclean, then *feel* unclean – yet you are clean in God's eyes! To fix this, we need to *cleanse ourselves from all filthiness of the flesh and spirit, perfecting holiness in the fear of God.*

How do we do this (and continue to do this) so the evil forces that surround us will not oppress us into submitting to the outer man and eventually to Satan himself? The answer is found in 1 John 1:7 where the Bible says, *But if we walk* [take repeated steps] *in the light* [spiritual direction], *as he is in the light, we have fellowship one with another, and the blood of Jesus Christ his Son cleanseth us from all sin.*

Now, don't get ahead of the verse and assume that we must re-cleanse ourselves whenever we step away from our spiritual direction. No, the blood of Christ has already done that. Being saved, the blood has cleansed us. But taking repeated steps in the light [spiritual direction from the Holy Spirit] will keep us in fellowship with God. If we are in fellowship with God, we cannot be in fellowship with devils. We cannot be oppressed by them when we walk in the light. First Corinthians 10:20-21 says, *I would not that ye should have fellowship with devils. Ye cannot drink the cup of the Lord, and the cup of devils: ye cannot be partakers of the Lord's table, and of the table of devils.*

Staying in the light of the Holy Spirit's leading will keep us from feeling unclean. Returning to that light will restore the broken fellowship between us and God in us. This will hinder the influence of outside oppression.

Whenever the oppressor wins, we are left thinking, acting, or feeling unclean. God can change all that. Our thinking can be *transformed* and our acting can be *conformed* into His image as we yield to the light of the inner man. We only need to take one step to feel better about ourselves: *confession*. You see, it is the devil's goal to keep us engaged in or dwelling on unconfessed sin to make us feel guilty, even though we are not guilty. If he can get us to do that, we will remain defeated. God can remove the guilty unclean feelings as well as the thoughts and actions. His remedy is found in 1 John 1:9: *If we confess our sins, he is faithful and just to forgive us our sins, and to cleanse us from all unrighteousness. Confess* means "to agree." If we agree with God that the soul is leading the body and that we are not under His influence (even though we are at times doing good) and ask Him to forgive us, we will be cleansed. He removes the guilt and shame that comes from not living under His control. What a blessed way to live!

Don't let the devil oppress you into thinking, acting, or feeling unclean. I have shared with you a biblical method for cleaning up your messes. Now you can be, as John 15:3 says, *clean through the word which I have spoken unto you.* Accept the blame for your actions and God will remove the guilt!

AFTERWORD

I am crucified with Christ: nevertheless I live; yet not I, but Christ liveth in me: and the life which I now live in the flesh I live by the faith of the Son of God, who loved me, and gave himself for me.— Galatians 2:20

As we come to the final page of this book, let us remember the theme of *Recovery through God's Truth*. The Christian life is not ours, it is Christ's. When we learn to live under His leading we will experience a life worth dying for. If you are holding onto the life that was crucified with Christ, let me encourage you to let it go and let God live His life through you. You won't ever need "will power" again. If you are willing, He will provide the power.

Just remember this truth: God is living in you. He is not only an influence, nor is He only a leading or only a revealer. He is a person. A living Person, the Holy Spirit! He is in you and you are not your own; He is now waiting to live through you. When this truth permeates every part of your conscience, you will see that the life you now live, you are living through the faith of the Son of God who gave Himself for you.

For to me to live is Christ, and to die is gain! — Philippians 1:21

MORE BOOKS BY STEVEN B. CURINGTON

THE UMBRELLA FELLA
(Code: CE-123 Price: $12.00)

Within every believer's heart is a desire to be all that God would have us to be. But, how can we be what God wants us to be, when we cannot even do the things God wants us to do?! The Umbrella Fella will help us understand our position in the Kingdom of Heaven's chain of command. Once we understand our position, it will forever change our disposition. It all begins with a two letter prepostion, the little word, IN.

TODAY I LAY (Code: CE-124 Price: $9.00)

Seldom does a day go by that we are not faced with opportunity the to die to self. Most every believer recognizes their personal responsibility to put their own wishes and wants on the altar and to sacrifice himself for the cause of Christ.

However, God expects much more than a daily dying to self in order to qualify for the power of His ressurection. For us to experience this supernatural power on our lives, we must be willing to not only die for Christ, but to die with Him, be buried with Him and then be raised to walk with Him as we engage in a regular evaluation of our DBR.

TALL LAW (Code: CE-117 Price: $12.00)

There are two types of Christian life - the abundant life and the redundant life. One is a life of restful service while the other is a life of discouraging works. How do you attain the real deal? You must understand the foundational truths of behavior modification. If you don't then you will have to live your life in your power rather that the power of God - and that's a mighty Tall Law.

WHY IS EVERYBODY CRYING
(Code: CE-118 Price: $7.00)

Most every Christian understands that they cannot be possessed. But yet they still find themselves doing things that make them sure the devil made them do it. How does this happen? Very simple... demonic oppression. Learn how Satan uses outside pressure (oppression) to render God's people discouraged and apathetic in their God-given responsibilities in life.

PRODUCE THE JUICE (Code: CE-121 Price: $16.00)

Produce the Juice references the motivational stimulation that a gifted believer experiences when the Holy Spirit exercises His gift(s) that He has placed within the believer. In this book Steve Curington shows how using your gift produces great joy and excitement in the life of a believer. (Comes with a spiritual gifts test CD)

JOURNALS AND CURRICULUM

PERSONAL RECOVERY KIT
(Code: KIT-001 Price: $99.00)

Behavior modification is needed by many people struggling from the results of conflicts and injuries obtained in today's society. This modification is not only needed because of the injuries but also the insults that we have added to those injuries in the form of addictions. This material written by the Founder of Reformers Unanimous is a biblical approach to overcoming both the insults and the injuries that so many are in bondage under. Follow the path that has set thousands free from bondage.

"IT'S PERSONAL" DAILY JOURNAL
(Code: CE-111 Price: $15.00)

The 90-day It's Personal Daily Journal is a proven method for developing a dynamic love-relationship with Jesus Christ. The journal is our #1 selling product in America! It comes complete with a CD explaining how to use the journal and its five forms of communication with God. (Classic size - 7 x 8 1/2)

COMPACT SIZE -"IT'S PERSONAL" DAILY JOURNAL (Code: CE-112 Price: $12.00)

Same classic journal, but in a new compact size! It fits easily into your purse or Bible cover. This 5" x 7" journal contains all five forms of communication. (30-day supply)

ADULT FULL SIZE- "IT'S PERSONAL" DAILY JOURNAL (Code: CE-116 Price: $17.00)

A larger version of our 90-day It's Personal Daily Journal is a proven method for developing a dynamic love-relationship with Jesus Christ. The journal is our #1 selling product in America! It comes complete with a CD explaining how to use the journal and its five forms of communication with God. (Full size - 8 1/2 x 11)

A STEVEN B. CURINGTON READING GUIDE

To exchange a redundant life for the abundant life.

Dealing with outside pressure properly.

Gaining God's power on your life.

Developing motivation to do more for God.

Learning to decrease that He might increase.